# 101 BEST WEB SITES

# for PRINCIPALS

### SECOND EDITION

Susan Brooks-Young

International Society for Technology in Education

EUGENE, OREGON • WASHINGTON, DC

# 101 BEST WEB SITES for PRINCIPALS SECOND EDITION

## Susan Brooks-Young

DIRECTOR OF PUBLISHING
Jean Marie Hall

ACQUISITIONS EDITOR
Scott Harter

PRODUCTION EDITOR
Tracy Cozzens

PRODUCTION COORDINATOR
Amy Miller

COPY EDITOR
Nancy Olson

BOOK DESIGN
Kim McGovern, Tracy Cozzens

COVER DESIGN
Kim McGovern

LAYOUT AND PRODUCTION
Tracy Cozzens

**International Society for Technology in Education (ISTE)**
Washington, DC, Headquarters:
    1710 Rhode Island Ave. NW, Suite 900, Washington, DC 20036-3132
Eugene, Oregon, Office:
    175 West Broadway, Suite 300, Eugene, OR 97401–3003
Order Desk: 1.800.336.5191
Order Fax: 1.541.302.3778
Customer Service: orders@iste.org
Book Publishing: books@iste.org
Rights and Permissions: permissions@iste.org
Web: www.iste.org

**Second Edition**
ISBN 978-1-56484-214-5

# ABOUT ISTE

The International Society for Technology in Education (ISTE) is a nonprofit professional organization with a worldwide membership of leaders in education technology. We are dedicated to promoting appropriate uses of technology to support and improve learning, teaching, and administration in PK–12 and teacher education. As part of that mission, ISTE provides high-quality and timely information, services, and materials, such as this book.

ISTE Book Publishing works with experienced educators to develop and produce practical resources for classroom teachers, teacher educators, and technology leaders. Every manuscript we select for publication is carefully peer-reviewed and professionally edited. We look for content that emphasizes the effective use of technology where it can make a difference—increasing the productivity of teachers and administrators; helping students with unique learning styles, abilities, or backgrounds; collecting and using data for decision making at the school and district levels; and creating dynamic, project-based learning environments that engage 21st-century learners. We value your feedback on this book and other ISTE products. E-mail us at **books@iste.org**.

ISTE is home of the National Educational Technology Standards (NETS) Project, the National Educational Computing Conference (NECC), and the National Center for Preparing Tomorrow's Teachers to Use Technology (NCPT3). To find out more about these and other ISTE initiatives and to view our complete book list or request a print catalog, visit our Web site at **www.iste.org**. You'll find information about:

- ISTE, our mission, and our members

- Membership opportunities and services

- Online communities and special interest groups (SIGs)

- Professional development services

- Research and evaluation services

- Educator resources

- ISTE's National Educational Technology Standards (NETS) for Students, Teachers, and Administrators

- *Learning & Leading with Technology* magazine

- *Journal of Research on Technology in Education*

# ABOUT THE AUTHOR

**Susan Brooks-Young** has been involved in instructional technology since 1979. She was one of the first teachers in her district to use technology in the classroom and has continued to explore ways it can be used for student learning. She has worked as a computer mentor, technology trainer, and technology curriculum specialist. As a site administrator, she continued to place a high priority on technology and in 1993 founded Computer Using Educators' (CUE) Administrators Special Interest Group, which still serves as a network and resource for school administrators in the United States and Canada.

Before establishing her own consulting firm, Susan was a teacher, site administrator, and technology specialist at a county office of education, a career that spanned more than 23 years. She now works with school districts and regional centers on technology-related issues, develops curriculum, presents workshops, teaches online courses, and writes articles for a variety of education journals.

Susan co-chairs ISTE's Special Interest Group for Administrators. She has also authored several popular books for school administrators who want to ensure that students and teachers can take full advantage of the unique capabilities of technology in the classroom. These titles, published by ISTE, include *Making Technology Standards Work for You: A Guide for School Administrators* (2002), *The Electronic Briefcase for Administrators: Tools and Templates* (2003), and *101 Best Web Sites for District Leaders* (2004).

# Contents

# Introduction

*"Logging on—what a laugh.*
        *They should have called it stepping off."*

—*DIRT MUSIC,* by Tim Winton (2001, Scribner)

I n the opening of the novel *Dirt Music*, Georgie Jutland muses about the six hours she has just lost wandering the Internet. While some folks love rambling from site to site, immersing themselves in cyberspace, most of us don't have the time or patience to devote to meandering searches that may or may not lead to the information we need. In fact, in his work with school administrators, professional development specialist Rick Fitzpatrick is finding that principals who can't locate what they're looking for in three or four clicks usually give up, then tend to discount the Internet as an unreliable source of information.

## HOW THIS BOOK CAN HELP YOU

Internet access has redefined my work style as a school administrator, as an author, and as a consultant; however, it was a slow and sometimes laborious process. The purpose of this book is to help school principals shortcut that process and to quickly become proficient Internet users. The second purpose of the book is to provide principals quick access to the best Internet sites available for their regular use.

The Internet directory itself is the meat of the book. You'll find 101 Web sites listed alphabetically within 12 categories. To help you find the best Web sites for a particular need, Quick Reference Charts are provided at the beginning of each category, showing the primary areas of emphasis for each site. Following the chart is a listing of each site, with the name and Internet address (URL), a screenshot, and a written summary that includes a site description and highlights for principals.

*Please note:* Within each summary, all **active links** appear in bold text. For ease of entering the listed URLs in your browser, we do not include the http:// prefix. All up-to-date Web browsers will autimatically add this after you type in the domain name.

If you're just getting started with the Internet, you'll want to review part 2, "Internet Survival Skills," before using part 1, "Directory of Internet Sites." Part 2 will help you understand hardware and software issues and explains the ins and outs of Web browsers. Chapter 3 of part 2, "Beyond the Basics," will help more experienced Internet surfers use more than one browser program, take advantage of multiple windows while online, organize favorites, and structure searches. Appendix C, the glossary, will also be helpful to new users.

There continues to be an increased focus on school administrators' technological skills. You may find yourself using this directory as text for a course or training session on using the Internet. Many districts are also asking principals to include a goal related to instructional technology in their annual professional-growth plans. Appendix A, National Educational Technology Standards for Administrators (NETS•A), and appendix B, Correlation to NETS•A, will help you identify how sites relate to NETS•A. This information is very helpful in completing coursework or professional-growth objectives aligned to the standards.

My primary hope is that the directory will be a valuable tool to assist busy principals in their daily work. With this reference, you'll have one more resource to turn to in your efforts to create strong programs for students and a positive working environment for both staff and yourself.

## WHEN YOU CAN'T FIND A LISTED SITE

Every effort has been made to ensure that the URLs and links provided are as accurate as possible. However, Web addresses change and so do specific link titles on individual pages. Following are tips for finding information when a change has been made.

Typically, when you enter an Internet address and see something unexpected, it's because you've made an error in entering the address, so check that first. However, if the address is correct, and the page doesn't provide the information or links you expect to see, try the following steps.

Trim the URL by eliminating some of the information at the end. For example, if the address **http://www.publicengagement.com/resources/standards/index.htm** doesn't work, try **http://www.publicengagement.com/resources/standards/**, then **http://www. publicengagement.com/resources/**, then **http://www.publicengagement.com/**, until you find a page you can access.

Once you open a page for the site, scan it for link titles or topics mentioned in the directory description. Sometimes the link titles may have been changed slightly; for example, **Community Collaboration Tools** might have been changed to **Standards Toolkit.** Click a title that seems to identify a similar topic, and you'll probably find what you're looking for.

Many Web sites also offer a search function. If the link titles don't look familiar, scroll through the page for a search option and enter the topic or link title provided in the directory. This should lead you to the information you need.

There may be times when you enter the Internet address correctly, trim it several times, and still get a message that the page is unavailable. In this case, it may be that the computer hosting the Web site is malfunctioning and you need to try again later. To double-check, try using a search engine to find the site, using the name provided in the directory. To try this, do the following: Enter the Internet address for a search engine such as Google (**www.google.com**). When the Google page appears, type the name of the Web site as provided in the directory and click on the Google Search button. Scroll through the results, and you should find a link to the page you want to access. Click on the link provided.

Sometimes sites do go down and stay down permanently. The sites selected for this directory were chosen because they're sponsored by reputable organizations that have a good track record for keeping sites current and online. If you find that a link simply doesn't work, please send an e-mail to **Web4Principals@aol.com**, and I'll try to help you find the site, or its equivalent.

SUSAN BROOKS-YOUNG

Curriculum

Data-Driven
Decision Making

Finance

General

Instruction

# PART 1

## DIRECTORY OF INTERNET SITES

Personal
Productivity

Professional
Development

Professional
Organizations

Professional
Reading

Research Institutes and
Education Centers

Social and Legal Issues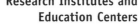

Technology Use

# Curriculum

During the last decade, standards-based curricula have become increasingly important in our schools. The No Child Left Behind Act of 2001 requires every state in the United States to develop academic standards and create an assessment program to measure student progress in meeting those standards. Ultimately, principals are the ones responsible for working with teachers to help them understand and implement the standards on a daily basis.

The Web sites in this section provide information on standards, suggestions for implementing standards-based curricula, and information on research about best practices. The section also includes links to major content-area groups such as the International Reading Association and the National Council for Teachers of Mathematics. Several former ERIC Clearinghouse sites that are now housed in different locations are included here. A new centralized ERIC site went online in September 2004. The URL for this site is **www.eric.ed.gov**. Because the site was not available for review during the revision of this book, it is not included in the listings provided below. You may also want to visit the Association for Supervision and Curriculum Development (ASCD) at **www.ascd.org**, listed in the Professional Organizations section of this directory.

| NAME OF SITE/INTERNET ADDRESS | PRIMARY AREA OF EMPHASIS | | | |
| --- | --- | --- | --- | --- |
| | CONTENT AREA | RESEARCH | PROFESSIONAL ORGANIZATION | STANDARDS |
| Achieve.org<br>www.achieve.org/achieve.nsf/home?openform | | | | ■ |
| Clearinghouse on Reading, English, & Communication<br>reading.indiana.edu | language arts | | | |
| Content Knowledge, Third Edition<br>www.mcrel.org/standards-benchmarks/ | all | | | ■ |
| Early Childhood and Parenting Collaborative<br>ecap.crc.uiuc.edu/info/ | | ■ | | |
| Educational REALMS<br>www.stemworks.org/realmshomepage.html | science, math, environment | ■ | | |
| Federal Resources for Educational Excellence (FREE)<br>www.ed.gov/free/ | all | | | |
| International Reading Association (IRA)<br>www.reading.org | language arts | | ■ | |
| MarcoPolo<br>www.marcopolo-education.org | all | | | ■ |
| National Council for the Social Studies (NCSS)<br>www.ncss.org or www.socialstudies.org | social science | | ■ | |
| National Council of Teachers of English (NCTE)<br>www.ncte.org | language arts | | ■ | ■ |
| National Council of Teachers of Mathematics (NCTM)<br>www.nctm.org | math | | ■ | ■ |
| National Science Teachers Association (NSTA)<br>www.nsta.org/administrators | science | | ■ | |
| No Child Left Behind<br>www.ed.gov/nclb/landing.jhtml?src=pb | all | ■ | | |
| Social Studies Development Center<br>www.indiana.edu/%7Essdc/ssdc.htm | social science, social studies | | | ■ |
| Standards and Accountability<br>www.publicengagement.com/resources/standards/ | | ■ | | ■ |

## Achieve.org

www.achieve.org/achieve.nsf/home?openform

**SITE DESCRIPTION.** Corporate leaders and the nation's governors formed Achieve Inc. in 1996. It's an independent, nonprofit, bipartisan organization that helps states raise academic standards, improve assessments, and increase accountability in schools. The site offers policy makers articles, publications, and tips on testing and accountability.

**HIGHLIGHTS FOR PRINCIPALS.** The **Call to Action** area examines two questions: **Why Standards?** and **Why Tests?** The two articles include links to supporting documentation and other resources. Check out **News/Reports** for free up-to-date articles and publications. Finally, whether you're involved in making policy decisions or carrying them out, you'll find helpful background material in **Policy Tips**.

## Clearinghouse on Reading, English, & Communication
**reading.indiana.edu**

**SITE DESCRIPTION.** Formerly the ERIC Clearinghouse for Reading, English, & Communication, the Clearinghouse on Reading, English, & Communication hosts many of the materials that were on the ERIC site. You'll find **News About Reading, Books & Bulletins, Lesson Plans,** a **Family Info Center, Online Education** opportunities, **Web Resources,** and access to the ERIC collection.

**HIGHLIGHTS FOR PRINCIPALS.** With today's emphasis on literacy, this site is a gold mine. Visit the **News About Reading** area to easily find the latest news and research on reading. As you provide support to teachers in instruction, refer them to the extensive lesson plan bank, categorized for quick access. The **Family Info Center** offers free brochures and other resources to use with parents, and the **Online Education** area has a free course for teaching phonics, along with a Phonics Toolkit for teachers in Grades K–3.

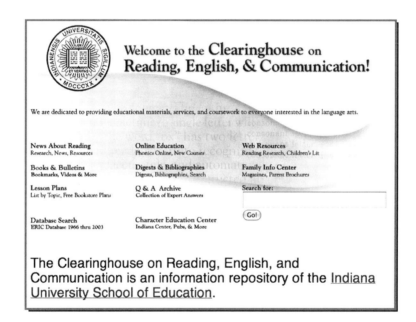

## Content Knowledge, Third Edition

www.mcrel.org/standards-benchmarks/

**SITE DESCRIPTION.** Mid-continent Research for Education and Learning (McREL), established in 1966, is a private, nonprofit organization whose purpose is to improve education through applied research and development. This particular link takes you directly to McREL's searchable standards database.

**HIGHLIGHTS FOR PRINCIPALS.** If you need quick access to national standards, this is a good place to look. You can browse the various content standards areas or use the search engine to find a particular standard. You'll also find examples of standards-based activities developed by McREL staff and links to other lesson plan sites. These provide good support for teachers who are polishing their skills in developing standards-based lessons and units of instruction.

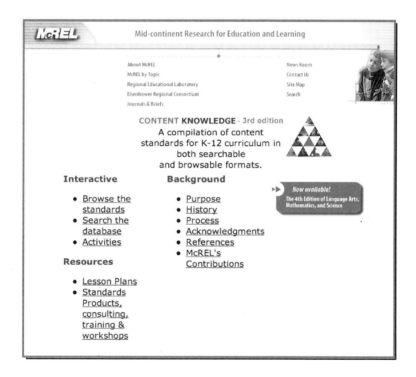

## Early Childhood and Parenting Collaborative

ecap.crc.uiuc.edu/info/

**SITE DESCRIPTION.** Formerly the ERIC Clearinghouse for Elementary and Early Childhood Education, the Early Childhood and Parenting Collaborative hosts many of the public domain materials that were on the ERIC/CEEP site. The **Publications** section of this site offers resources from the clearinghouse and several other projects.

**HIGHLIGHTS FOR PRINCIPALS.** An online publication you'll want to review and use is *Early Childhood Research and Practice (ECRP)*. Published twice annually, *ECRP* contains useful information for staff and parents. You can download these publications for easy distribution. Access *ECRP* in the **Publications** section by clicking on **Publications page** and then on the **ECRP** link. **Popular Topics** is also accessible here and provides links to timely information and program models on parenting, early literacy, and school readiness. Illinois Early Learning Project **Tip Sheets** (on the main **Publications** page) offer a wealth of information as well.

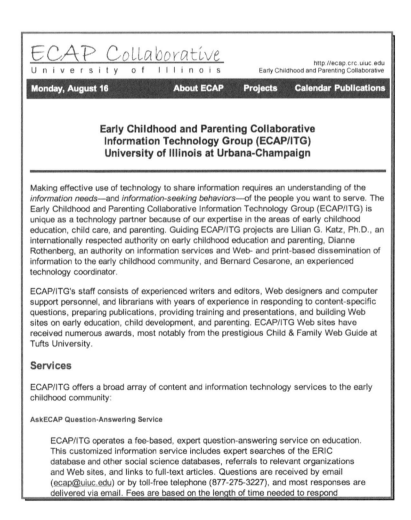

## Educational REALMS

www.stemworks.org/realmshomepage.html

**SITE DESCRIPTION.** Formerly the ERIC Clearinghouse for Science, Mathematics, and Environmental Education (ERIC/CSMEE), Educational REALMS hosts many of the public domain materials that were on the ERIC/CSMEE site. Browse this site by clicking on various resource types listed on the home page.

**HIGHLIGHTS FOR PRINCIPALS.** The **Bulletins** and **Digests** include many articles and briefs related to research and trends in math and science education. These are good resources when you need information quickly. You may want to share the **Web Companions** area with teachers. These annotated collections of Web resources are designed to help science teachers find quality online resources.

## Federal Resources for Educational Excellence

**www.ed.gov/free/**

**SITE DESCRIPTION.** More than 30 federal agencies make teaching and learning resources for all major content areas available through the Federal Resources for Educational Excellence (FREE) Web site. The site is updated each month.

**HIGHLIGHTS FOR PRINCIPALS.** Use this site to help your teachers find support materials and resources. The content area links and the **More For Students** both include a wide variety of materials. When visiting the **What is FREE?** area, be sure to click on the **CE toolkit** link on the left. These downloadable resources may be used to guide teachers who want to learn more about technology integration.

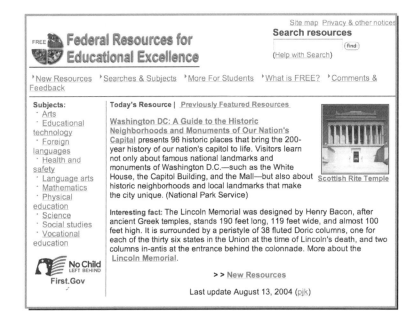

## International Reading Association

**www.reading.org**

**SITE DESCRIPTION.** The International Reading Association (IRA) promotes high levels of literacy through quality reading instruction and makes available research and other information concerning literacy. The site is a resource for professional development opportunities, links to literacy resources, and archives of articles and other information.

**HIGHLIGHTS FOR PRINCIPALS.** The home page features a list of valuable links under Online Resources. Visit the **Focus on Topics in Reading** link for focus pages that offer concise information about specific reading issues. For example, current topics include pages about adolescent literacy, critical literacy, the No Child Left Behind Act, and reading assessment. This area makes it easy for you to keep up-to-date with reading issues. Also visit **Literacy Links** for quick access to quality Web sites that address literacy concerns.

## MarcoPolo

**www.marcopolo-education.org**

**SITE DESCRIPTION.** MarcoPolo provides free K–12 standards-based Internet lessons, activities, and materials designed to help teachers integrate technology into their classrooms. The site also offers information about professional development opportunities.

**HIGHLIGHTS FOR PRINCIPALS.** The **Teacher Resources** area is rich with materials you can share with your staff. Here are some of the resources for you to review and share (click **more** to see the full list):

- **MarcoPolo Content:** Lessons, Featured Resources, Standards Alignment

- **How to Use MarcoPolo:** Classroom Integration, Types of Internet Content, Technology Tips

- **MarcoPolo Resources:** MarcoGrams, Guides & Materials

## National Council for the Social Studies

**www.ncss.org** or **www.socialstudies.org**

**SITE DESCRIPTION.** The purpose of the National Council for the Social Studies (NCSS) organization is to provide leadership, service, and support to social studies educators. The areas most useful to principals are:

- **About NCSS:** Position Statements

- **Your Classroom:** Notable Trade Books for Young People

- **Advocacy:** Legislative Update

**HIGHLIGHTS FOR PRINCIPALS.** You can quickly access information about federal legislation as it relates to teaching social studies or review position statements addressing important issues in social studies education. You can also download bibliographies of trade books reviewed and recommended for use with students in Grades PK–8. These book lists date back to 2000.

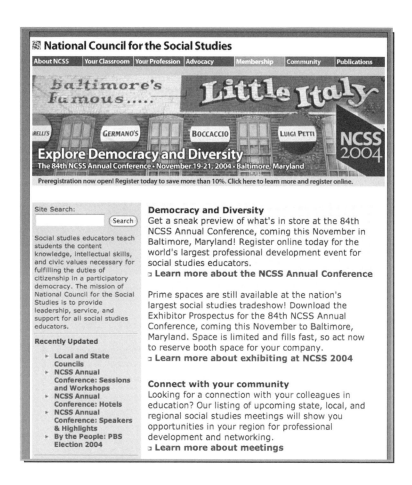

## National Council of Teachers of English

**www.ncte.org**

**SITE DESCRIPTION.** The National Council of Teachers of English (NCTE) promotes improvement in the teaching and learning of English and the language arts. The two areas most helpful for principals are **About NCTE** and **Programs**.

**HIGHLIGHTS FOR PRINCIPALS. About NCTE** contains more than organizational information. You'll also find useful links to education **Issues** and **Research**. In addition, NCTE offers a variety of programs designed to address special areas of concern such as intellectual freedom. Links to extensive information about each of these are provided on the **Programs** page. You may view information by scholastic level as well (use the drop-down menu to select).

# National Council of Teachers of Mathematics

**www.nctm.org**

**SITE DESCRIPTION.** The National Council of Teachers of Mathematics (NCTM) strives to ensure that all students receive a high-quality mathematics education. The site offers information about **NCTM Standards**, publications, and resources (for elementary school, middle school, and high school).

**HIGHLIGHTS FOR PRINCIPALS.** Visit the **Leaders** section of the site from the link at the bottom of the page. Here you'll find pointers to items of interest for school administrators. For example, you can easily access NCTM position statements, legislative and policy updates, and articles of interest to administrators.

## National Science Teachers Association

**www.nsta.org/administrators**

**SITE DESCRIPTION.** The National Science Teachers Association (NSTA) works to promote excellence and innovation in the teaching of science. The site offers a wealth of information for teachers of science, kindergarten through postsecondary, and targets areas of interest to school administrators through the specific link provided here.

**HIGHLIGHTS FOR PRINCIPALS.** Although you may want to visit other areas of the NSTA site, begin with the **Administrators** page to find the most helpful information for principals. Topics include:

- **Teacher recognition programs**
- **Student competitions**
- **Building a Presence for Science**
- **Position statements**
- **SciLinks**
- **Science Education Suppliers Guide**

Many principals will want to begin with the last three areas listed.

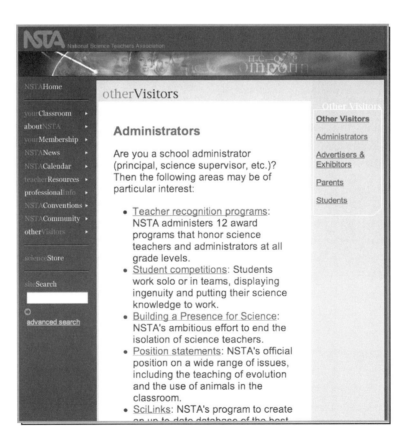

## No Child Left Behind

**www.ed.gov/nclb/landing.jhtml?src=pb**

**SITE DESCRIPTION.** This is the official U.S. Department of Education Web site for the No Child Left Behind Act. Topics include **NCLB Guidance**, **NCLB Update**, **K–12 Education Funding**, and more. Also try the **Administrators** link at the top of the page.

**HIGHLIGHTS FOR PRINCIPALS.** The *No Child Left Behind: A Toolkit for Teachers* booklet contains important information about NCLB and teacher quality. A related publication, *No Child Left Behind: A Parents Guide,* answers frequently asked questions about the impact of NCLB on public schools. (From the main page, click on **Teachers Toolkit**, **Parents Guide**, to access both). Both can be downloaded as PDFs. Sign up for **Extra Credit & The Achiever**, free e-newsletters that provide regular updates on NCLB. The **NCLB Guidance** area offers links to explanations of NCLB policies.

## Social Studies Development Center
**www.indiana.edu/%7Essdc/ssdc.htm**

**SITE DESCRIPTION.** Formerly the ERIC Clearinghouse for Social Studies/Social Science Education, the Social Studies Development Center hosts many of the public domain materials that were on the clearinghouse site. Browse by clicking on various resource types listed on the home page. Five separate sections enable you to search digests, visit Web sites related to social studies and social science, and access academic standards.

**HIGHLIGHTS FOR PRINCIPALS.** The **Social Studies Standards and Curriculum Frameworks** link takes you to an area where you can access both national and state standards for social studies, art, and music. The **SSDC Digests** link provides access to the full text of these publications from 1996 to 2003. Many of the topics addressed are of interest to principals and teachers. You may also want to share the **Links to Other Internet Social Studies Resources** with teaching staff.

## Standards and Accountability

**www.publicengagement.com/resources/standards/**

**SITE DESCRIPTION.** The Collaborative Communications Group worked with school districts in California, Texas, and Kentucky to develop the **Standards Toolkit**. Click on **Standards & Accountability** in the menu on the left, then **Resources** at the bottom of the introduction, then the link in the first paragraph. Within the toolkit, topics covered are:

- **Engaging Parents:** Suggestions and materials for presenting standards-based instruction to parents through back-to-school nights, open houses, parent forums, and other meetings (a $10 video may be ordered for use with parents).

- **Explaining Standards:** A PowerPoint slideshow available for downloading, as well as sample brochures for parents

- **Changing Practice:** Information on two videos ($10 each), along with a downloadable report, for use with staff. Also, tools specifically for principals, including bibliographies, guidelines for observing literacy lessons, and a communication packet

- **Assessing Achievement:** Tools for teachers to use to evaluate student writing and create math portfolios

- **Reporting Progress:** Information on standards-based report cards and student-led conferencing

**HIGHLIGHTS FOR PRINCIPALS.** Although the target audience is middle school administrators, elementary and high school principals will also find useful information and good ideas here. Be sure to review the ideas in the toolkit for parent meetings and communication. You may also want to read and share the article "No Child Left Behind: New Expectations, New Options, New Opportunities for Parents to be Involved," found in the **Resources** area.

# Data-Driven
# Decision Making

C oined relatively recently, the term data-driven decision making
is now ubiquitous in discussions about curriculum and
instructional design. The No Child Left Behind Act requires
districts to gather and report data about student performance in
relation to academic standards. It also requires prescriptive, research-
based interventions when student academic achievement is below par.

The Web sites in this section provide an overview of standardized
testing, including its strengths and weaknesses, what the scores mean,
and strategies for working with staff to make programmatic decisions
based on the student data gathered. In particular, "Thinking About
Tests and Testing: A Short Primer in 'Assessment Literacy'" and The
ToolBelt offered by the North Central Regional Educational Laboratory
(NCREL) provide ready-to-use practical tools and information.

# QUICK REFERENCE CHART

| NAME OF SITE/INTERNET ADDRESS | PRIMARY AREA OF EMPHASIS | | | | | |
|---|---|---|---|---|---|---|
| | UNDER-STANDING TESTING | SPECIFIC TEST INFORMA-TION | PERFOR-MANCE REPORTS | EVALUATION DESIGN | STUDENTS WITH SPECIAL NEEDS | ARTICLES AND BROCHURES |
| National Assessment Governing Board (NAGB) **www.nagb.org** | | ■ | ■ | | | ■ |
| National Center for Research on Evaluation, Standards, and Student Testing (CRESST) **www.cse.ucla.edu** | | ■ | | ■ | | ■ |
| National Center on Educational Outcomes (NCEO) **education.umn.edu/nceo/** | | | | | ■ | |
| School Information Partnership **www.schoolresults.org** | | | ■ | | | |
| Student Data Handbook for Elementary, Secondary, and Early Childhood Education **nces.ed.gov/pubsearch/ pubsinfo.asp?pubid=2000343r** | ■ | | | ■ | | |
| Thinking About Tests and Testing: A Short Primer in "Assessment Literacy" **www.aypf.org/subcats/repubs.htm** | ■ | | | | | |
| The ToolBelt **www.ncrel.org/toolbelt/** | | | | ■ | | ■ |

## National Assessment Governing Board

www.nagb.org

**SITE DESCRIPTION.** Congress created the 26-member National Assessment Governing Board (NAGB) in 1988. This independent, bipartisan group sets policy for the National Assessment of Educational Progress (NAEP).

**HIGHLIGHTS FOR PRINCIPALS.** The downloadable frameworks in the **Publications** section describe what students should know and be able to master at Grades 4, 8, and 12. The frameworks are not a curriculum but describe what the national assessment program will test. Content areas addressed are reading, writing, mathematics, science, arts education, foreign language, U.S. history, geography, and civics. Achievement level reports, other NAGB reports, and framework brochures are also available. To learn more about policies NAGB has adopted to implement the No Child Left Behind Act, click on the **NAGB** link, then the **Recent NAGB Policies** link.

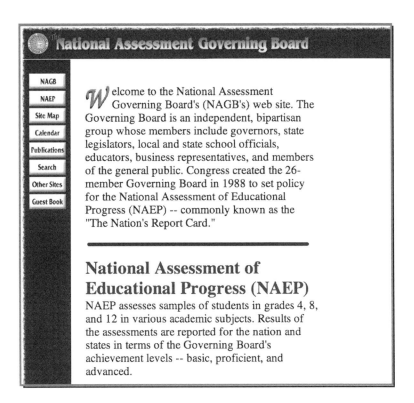

## National Center for Research on Evaluation, Standards, and Student Testing
www.cse.ucla.edu

**SITE DESCRIPTION.** The National Center for Research on Evaluation, Standards, and Student Testing (CRESST) focuses on the assessment of education programs, the design of assessments, and the validity of inferences drawn from assessment. Areas of greatest interest for principals are:

- **Newsletters:** Articles about topics related to accountability and CRESST research findings

- **Policy Briefs:** Information on current subjects including No Child Left Behind

- **Parents Page:** Assessment information for parents of K–12 children

- **Teachers Page:** Assessment information for teachers of K–12 children

**HIGHLIGHTS FOR PRINCIPALS.** Visit the links listed above to browse and download CRESST articles and policy briefs about assessment. The **Glossary**, which is accessed in the **Inside CRESST** drop-down menu is a handy tool for sharing common terminology with teachers and parents. Materials in the parent and teacher areas include articles, presentations, sample rubrics, and performance assignments.

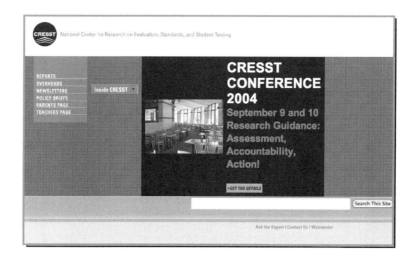

# National Center on Educational Outcomes

education.umn.edu/nceo/

**SITE DESCRIPTION.** Founded in 1990, the National Center on Educational Outcomes (NCEO) provides leadership in designing and creating assessment and accountability systems appropriate for all students, including those with disabilities or with limited English proficiency. Special topic areas are:

- Accommodations
- Accountability
- Alternate Assessments
- Graduation Requirements
- LEP Students
- Out-of-Level Testing
- Participation
- Reporting
- Standards
- Universal Design

**HIGHLIGHTS FOR PRINCIPALS.** The emphasis on testing *all* students makes it critical that principals have a clear understanding of how to proceed with those students who have special needs. This site answers basic questions about testing these students. It provides links to every state, giving you even more specific information about the requirements you must work under. You can also download reports and PowerPoint presentations about assessment and students with special needs.

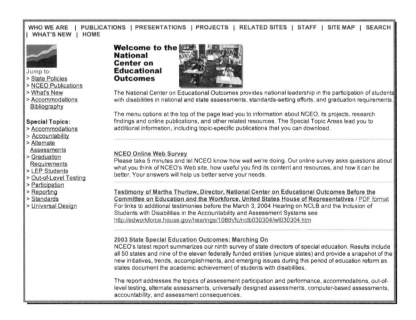

## School Information Partnership

**www.schoolresults.org**

**SITE DESCRIPTION.** The School Information Partnership, funded by the Broad Foundation and the U.S. Department of Education, makes readily available to parents and educators the data that must be publicly reported under the No Child Left Behind Act. The tools and data analysis offered through the site are intended to complement existing state data collection and analysis.

**HIGHLIGHTS FOR PRINCIPALS.** A U.S. map is prominently displayed on the home page. Click on your state and search for your individual school. In addition to Quick Facts about your school's adequate yearly progress (AYP), you can access a **Data Snapshot** for your school, in-depth AYP information, and analyses of student performance by grade level and enrollment. Several online tools will also allow you to compare your school's results with district and state results.

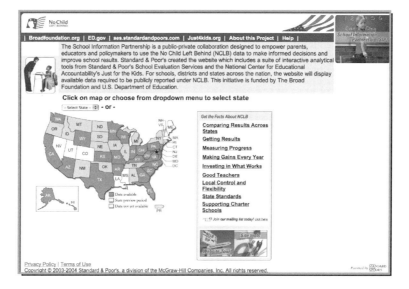

## Student Data Handbook for Elementary, Secondary, and Early Childhood Education

nces.ed.gov/pubsearch/pubsinfo.asp?pubid=2000343r

**SITE DESCRIPTION.** This link takes you to a page where you can download and print a copy of the *Student Data Handbook for Elementary, Secondary, and Early Childhood Education*. Both the original handbook and the 2001 update are included. It's also possible to order a print copy, if you prefer. This document is offered by the National Center for Education Statistics (NCES).

**HIGHLIGHTS FOR PRINCIPALS.** With the increased emphasis on data-driven decision making and assessment, this document is a valuable resource for school principals. The handbook defines student data elements, makes recommendations for building a student record system, discusses automated student record keeping, and refers readers to related NCES documents.

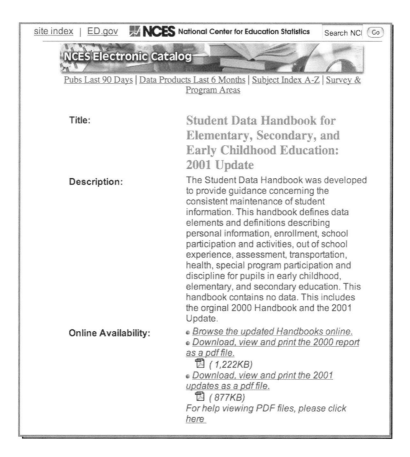

## Thinking about Tests and Testing:
## A Short Primer in "Assessment Literacy"

www.aypf.org/subcats/repubs.htm

**SITE DESCRIPTION.** This link takes you to the Publications on Research and Evaluation page of the American Youth Policy Forum (AYPF) site. Several reports here relate to academic achievement and are of interest to principals.

**HIGHLIGHTS FOR PRINCIPALS.** Scroll down the page to the link for **Thinking about Tests and Testing: A Short Primer in "Assessment Literacy,"** by Gerald W. Bracey. This primer is divided into three parts. Part I explains basic statistical terms educators need to understand when discussing testing. Part II focuses on test-specific terms. Part III discusses testing issues. The primer is an excellent tool for your own use and when working with teachers to help them understand how tests can be used to measure student performance.

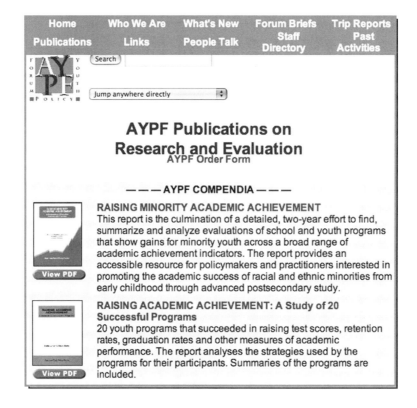

## The ToolBelt

**www.ncrel.org/toolbelt/**

**SITE DESCRIPTION.** The North Central Regional Educational Laboratory (NCREL) provides tools to help educators gather information about classrooms, schools, districts, professional practice, and the community. The ToolBelt includes checklists and surveys. Some should be printed and completed offline while others can be completed online. The site also includes information about how to make decisions using the data collected.

**HIGHLIGHTS FOR PRINCIPALS.** After clicking on the **Tools** link, you'll find **Data Analysis Tools**; **Regional**, **State and District Report Cards**; **Technology**; **Planning**; and **Supplemental Inventories**. Check out the links under each to see models for collecting and handling data and to access tools you can use at your site during data collection, analysis, and planning.

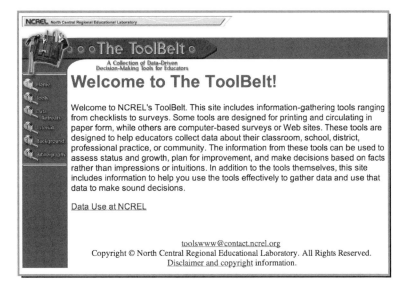

# Finance

**F**unding is an issue for every school. Either you don't have enough money and are constantly on the lookout for additional funds or you have many categorical funds at your disposal and must track and account for purchases to ensure that you and your staff are following the spending guidelines for various funding sources.

The Web sites listed here provide basic information about both school finance and education finance data (handy for grants and evaluations). You'll also find information about seeking additional funding through grant-writing or fund-raising activities.

# QUICK REFERENCE CHART

| NAME OF SITE/INTERNET ADDRESS | PRIMARY AREA OF EMPHASIS | | | |
|---|---|---|---|---|
| | PROGRAM INFORMATION | DATA | GRANTS/GRANT WRITING | FUND-RAISING |
| Education Commission of the States: Finance www.ecs.org/ecsmain.asp?page=/html/issuesK12.asp | ■ | | ■ | |
| Education Finance Database www.ncsl.org/programs/educ/ed_finance/ | ■ | ■ | | |
| Education Finance Statistics Center Publications nces.ed.gov/edfin/publications/pubs.asp | ■ | ■ | | |
| Federal, State, and Local Governments Public Elementary-Secondary Education Finance Data www.census.gov/govs/www/school.html | | ■ | | |
| Grants and Contests techlearning.com/resources/grants.jhtml | | | ■ | ■ |
| School Finance: From Equity to Adequacy www.mcrel.org/PDF/PolicyBriefs/5042PI_PBSchoolFinanceBrief.pdf | ■ | | | |
| School Finance Project www.wcer.wisc.edu/cpre/finance/ | ■ | ■ | | |
| School Fund-Raising Activities That Work teacher.scholastic.com/professional/grants/school_fund_raising.htm | | | | ■ |
| SchoolGrants www.schoolgrants.org | | | ■ | ■ |
| U.S. Department of Education: Budget Office www.ed.gov/about/overview/budget/index.html?src=gu | | ■ | ■ | |

## Education Commission of the States: Finance

**www.ecs.org/ecsmain.asp?page=/html/issuesK12.asp**

**SITE DESCRIPTION.** This link takes you to the K–12 Issues page of the Education Commission of the States (ECS) site. Click on the drop-down menu (labeled **Click here to select an issue**), scroll down to select **Finance**, and click **Go**.

**HIGHLIGHTS FOR PRINCIPALS.** This very readable overview of current school finance issues includes such topics as:

- **Equity**
- **Facilities**
- **Funding Formulas**

You'll also find links to information about special education and finance and to the Committee for Economic Development report, "Investing in Learning: School Funding Policies to Foster High Performance."

## Education Finance Database

**www.ncsl.org/programs/educ/ed_finance/**

**SITE DESCRIPTION.** The National Conference of State Legislatures maintains this Web site, which offers a searchable database of funding programs for each of the 50 states. Information includes local taxing methods, spending limits, earmarked state revenues, foundation program information, categorical funds, and recent litigation.

**HIGHLIGHTS FOR PRINCIPALS.** Do you understand how your state funds the basic per pupil allocation? Want to refresh your memory regarding categorical funds available in your state? Are you writing a grant that requires information about your state's funding program? The searchable database can help you find answers to these questions and many more.

## Education Finance Statistics Center Publications

nces.ed.gov/edfin/publications/pubs.asp

**SITE DESCRIPTION.** This site provides a listing of free publications available from the U.S. Department of Education and addresses various topics related to school finance.

**HIGHLIGHTS FOR PRINCIPALS.** Did you know you can order free single copies of reports from the U.S. Department of Education by calling 1.877.433.7827 or e-mailing **EdPubs@inet.ed.gov**? Twenty-nine titles are currently available and include:

- *Statistics in Brief: Revenues and Expenditures by Public School Districts: School Year 2000–01*

- *Characteristics of the 100 Largest Public Elementary and Secondary School Districts in the United States: 2000–01*

- *Developments in School Finance: 2001–02*

These reports are also available for downloading.

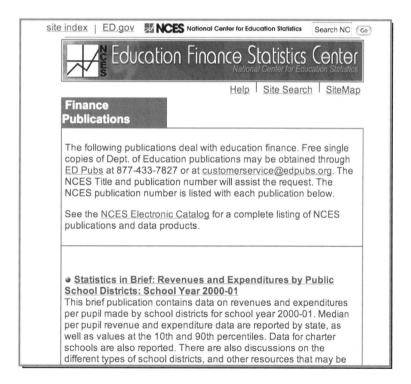

## Federal, State, and Local Governments Public Elementary-Secondary Education Finance Data

www.census.gov/govs/www/school.html

**SITE DESCRIPTION.** The Elementary-Secondary Education Statistics Branch, Governments Division, of the U.S. Census Bureau maintains this site. Finance data available on K–12 public school systems include:

- revenues
- expenditures
- debts
- assets

The data available are for years 1992–2002, with data for 2003 available in early 2005. The site is updated annually.

**HIGHLIGHTS FOR PRINCIPALS.** Summary tables are available for national and statewide reports, as well as for large school districts. You can also access data for individual school districts through downloadable files. This kind of information can be useful when applying for grants or when comparing your district's financial data with that of similar school districts nationally.

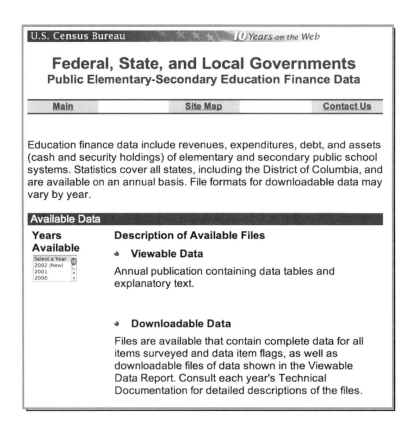

## Grants and Contests

**techlearning.com/resources/grants.jhtml**

**SITE DESCRIPTION.** This searchable, funding-source database provided by tech-LEARNING is updated monthly. In addition to listing grant and contest opportunities, the site provides several online articles with advice about writing grants.

**HIGHLIGHTS FOR PRINCIPALS.** Search the database using keywords or browse all the listings. All entries relate to education initiatives, and while many point to technology funds, other kinds of education programs are included. Look for the **Grants Directory** available in the **Also See...** column. Published annually, the directory highlights available grants month by month.

## School Finance: From Equity to Adequacy

www.mcrel.org/PDF/PolicyBriefs/5042PI_PBSchoolFinanceBrief.pdf

**SITE DESCRIPTION.** This link takes you directly to a PDF file. You need a copy of the free program Adobe Reader to download and read this file. If you do not have this program, go to **www.adobe.com/products/acrobat/readermain.html** to download and install the file. A more detailed description can be found in the Personal Productivity section of this directory.

**HIGHLIGHTS FOR PRINCIPALS.** This policy brief from Mid-continent Research for Education and Learning (McREL) looks at a recent shift in legal challenges to state school finance systems. For years, the focus of litigation has been equity. Now many lawsuits are addressing the need to provide higher levels of funding for all students (adequacy). The report reviews legal cases and provides guidelines for proactively addressing adequacy issues.

---

**McREL** **P O L I C Y** *brief*

*March 2004*

### School Finance: From Equity to Adequacy
*by Laura Lefkowits*

Equality has been a mantra of American public education since the common school was founded in the 19th century. The notion that all citizens are entitled to a free public education in order to gain sufficient knowledge to govern themselves and to contribute to a productive economy is a foundation principle of our democracy. Over the years, however, Americans have deliberated over what level of education is sufficient and who is responsible for providing the resources necessary to deliver it.

Policymakers, educators, parents, and other taxpayers have long engaged in debates about school funding systems. At times these disputes have found their way to court. Since the 1970s, school finance lawsuits have been filed in nearly every state, including each of the seven states in the Central Region.

*By taking a proactive approach to improving school finance systems, education leaders and policymakers may be able to minimize or avoid litigation and the sometimes costly and unworkable solutions that accompany court decisions.*

---

## School Finance Project

**www.wcer.wisc.edu/cpre/finance/**

**SITE DESCRIPTION.** The Consortium for Policy Research in Education (CPRE) conducts and facilitates research on a variety of school funding issues. Of particular interest to principals is the CPRE School Finance project. The focus of this project is to examine the cost of school-improvement and professional development initiatives. The site is a resource for articles, case studies, models, and a variety of other useful information.

**HIGHLIGHTS FOR PRINCIPALS.** Several sections are of interest to principals. For example:

- **Research:** Access to information on the analysis of costs of instructional improvements, resource reallocation, school-based budgeting, and how to determine the adequacy of funding programs

- **State/District Information:** Descriptions of each state's finance program and links to state departments of education

- **School Redesign Reports:** A free service to help you determine if your school can afford comprehensive reform designs

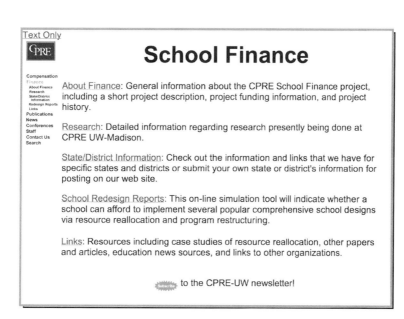

## School Fund-Raising Activities That Work

teacher.scholastic.com/professional/grants/school_fund_raising.htm

**SITE DESCRIPTION.** This link takes you to an article written by Gary Carnow about successful fund-raising activities, most of which do not include door-to-door selling and are not terribly labor intensive.

**HIGHLIGHTS FOR PRINCIPALS.** If you're looking for alternatives to candy and gift-wrap sales, read this article. Suggested fund-raising events include walk-a-thons, book fairs, academic marathons, and rummage sales. If you do want to sell merchandise, you'll find suggestions about scheduling and locating the best deal for your school.

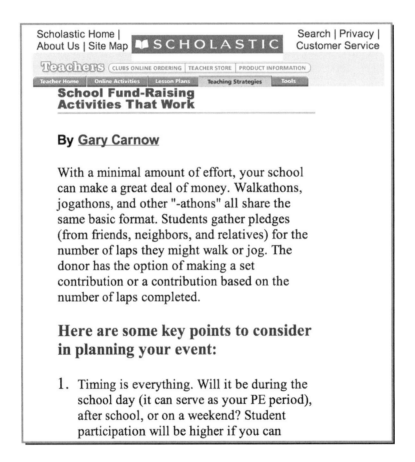

# SchoolGrants

**www.schoolgrants.org**

**SITE DESCRIPTION.** Established in 1999, this site offers information on how to write grants, as well as grant-writing opportunities.

**HIGHLIGHTS FOR PRINCIPALS.** A visit to the **Grant Writing Tips** section leads to basic information that helps grant writers develop successful proposals, hire consultants as grant writers, compose letters of inquiry, and evaluate proposals. **Grant Opportunities** is organized according to federal, state, and foundation opportunities. Check here for information and ideas about possible funding sources.

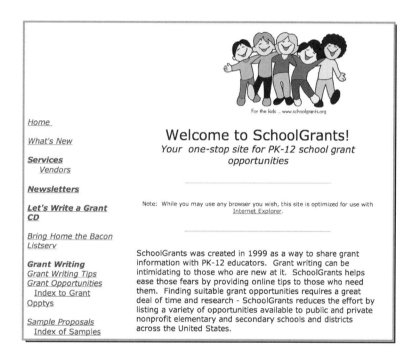

For the kids ... www.schoolgrants.org

### Welcome to SchoolGrants!
*Your one-stop site for PK-12 school grant opportunities*

Home

What's New

**Services**
Vendors

**Newsletters**

**Let's Write a Grant CD**

Bring Home the Bacon Listserv

**Grant Writing**
Grant Writing Tips
Grant Opportunities
  Index to Grant Opptys

Sample Proposals
  Index of Samples

Note: While you may use any browser you wish, this site is optimized for use with Internet Explorer.

SchoolGrants was created in 1999 as a way to share grant information with PK-12 educators. Grant writing can be intimidating to those who are new at it. SchoolGrants helps ease those fears by providing online tips to those who need them. Finding suitable grant opportunities requires a great deal of time and research - SchoolGrants reduces the effort by listing a variety of opportunities available to public and private nonprofit elementary and secondary schools and districts across the United States.

## U.S. Department of Education: Budget Office

**www.ed.gov/about/overview/budget/index.html?src=gu**

**SITE DESCRIPTION.** The Budget Office home page for the U.S. Department of Education spotlights the president's current education budget request, tracks congressional action on the department's budget, and explains the federal budget process. The site also offers tables on critical information such as state allocations and historic funding levels.

**HIGHLIGHTS FOR PRINCIPALS.** Making applications for federal funds may be a district responsibility. However, principals who understand the federal budget process and are aware of funding possibilities are in a better position both to make projections when developing their site budgets and to ensure that all appropriate funding sources are being tapped. This page also offers a link to two electronic **ED newsletters** (EDInfo and ED RSS), which regularly provide funding updates and information.

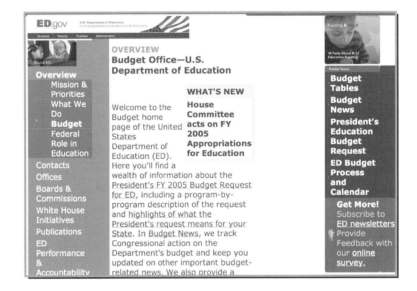

# General

Although they've developed gradually, some Web sites now either bill themselves as being specifically for school administrators or have designated areas for school administrators. The resources they provide target issues from an administrator's point of view and cover a broad range of topics. In addition to articles and links to other Web pages, several of the sites listed in this section include online networking opportunities via discussion boards, chat rooms, and e-mail lists.

# QUICK REFERENCE CHART

| NAME OF SITE/INTERNET ADDRESS | PRIMARY AREA OF EMPHASIS | | | |
|---|---|---|---|---|
| | DISCUSSION | CHAT | WEB PORTAL | PUBLICATIONS |
| AOL@School Administrators<br>**www.aolatschool.com/administrators/** | ■ | ■ | ■ | |
| Clearinghouse on Educational Policy and Management (CEPM)<br>**eric.uoregon.edu** | | | | ■ |
| e-Lead: Leadership for Student Learning<br>**www.e-lead.org** | | | | ■ |
| National Library of Education<br>**www.ed.gov/NLE/** | | | ■ | ■ |
| School Administrators Center<br>**www.education-world.com/a_admin/** | ■ | | | ■ |
| TeAch-nology<br>**www.teach-nology.com/edleadership/** | | | ■ | |
| U.S. Department of Education<br>**www.ed.gov** | | | | ■ |

## AOL@School Administrators

**www.aolatschool.com/administrators/**

**SITE DESCRIPTION.** America Online hosts this area as part of the AOL@School Web site. This site is actually a portal offering links to other Web sites. School site administrators will be interested in the sections listed in the left-hand column:

- **Curriculum & Standards**
- **Library & Media**
- **Professional Development**
- **Productivity Tools & Tips**
- **Education News**
- **Research & Reference**

Chat and discussion boards are also available.

**HIGHLIGHTS FOR PRINCIPALS.** A portal can be useful when you don't have time to conduct your own search for Web sites. Simply click on the topic you're interested in, select from the subcategories listed, and you'll find several Web sites to visit directly from this page.

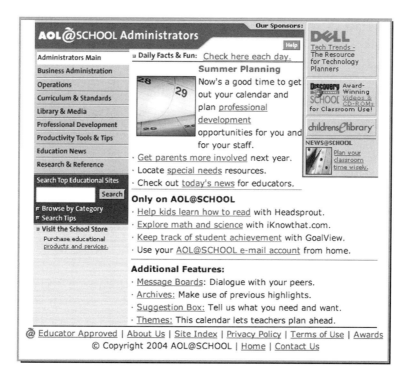

## Clearinghouse on Educational Policy and Management

### eric.uoregon.edu

**SITE DESCRIPTION.** Once a part of the Educational Resources Information Center (ERIC) system, this site is now maintained and updated by the College of Education at the University of Oregon. You can browse this collection by clicking on titles listed in such areas as:

- Trends & Issues
- Hot Topics
- Publications
- Directory of Organizations
- Search/Find

You'll also find links to related Web sites.

**HIGHLIGHTS FOR PRINCIPALS.** The **Hot Topics** and **Trends & Issues** areas are very helpful. **Hot Topics** pulls together quick links and resources from throughout the site that relate to front-burner issues such as class size or charter schools. **Trends & Issues** goes into more depth and typically includes three sections: **Discussion**, **References**, and **Resources**. Some also include article abstracts. Topics include the role of the school leader, labor relations, and more.

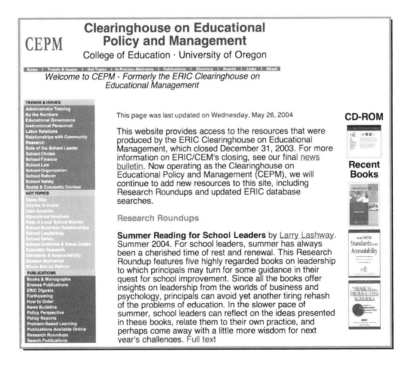

## e-Lead: Leadership for Student Learning

**www.e-lead.org**

**SITE DESCRIPTION.** This site connects principals to useful information for the development of their own leadership skills. In addition to learning about designing quality leadership development strategies, users can access a database of leadership programs and a library of resources.

**HIGHLIGHTS FOR PRINCIPALS.** The **Library** is especially useful for principals seeking support for their own professional growth. Select a topic of interest such as **Data-Driven Decision Making** or **Instructional Leadership**. Read the topic overview and click the link at the bottom of the page. This leads to a collection of resources, including more in-depth descriptions of the topic, tools and resources, model programs, and articles and research.

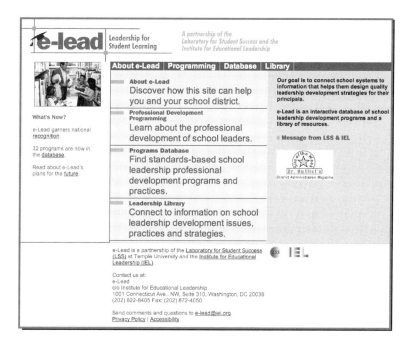

## National Library of Education

**www.ed.gov/NLE/**

**SITE DESCRIPTION.** This is the largest federally funded education library in the nation. Through this link you can access:

- **GEM:** The Gateway to Educational Materials provides one-step access to online lesson plans, curriculum units, and other resources.

- **VRD:** The Virtual Reference Desk is an Internet-based question-and-answer service that connects you to experts who can provide information and support.

- **ERIC:** The Educational Information Resources Center links to the new, centralized bibliographic database.

- **NCEF:** The National Clearinghouse for Educational Facilities provides information about all aspects of K–12 school facilities, from planning through construction, operations, and maintenance.

- **USNEI:** The United States Network for Education Information is an information and referral system for educators, parents, and students to learn about international education.

- **Ed Pubs:** This links you to the U.S. Department of Education's online ordering system for the department's publications and other products.

**HIGHLIGHTS FOR PRINCIPALS.** This resource can link you to almost any government-produced educational material you might want.

## School Administrators Center

**www.education-world.com/a_admin/**

**SITE DESCRIPTION.** Education World hosts an area strictly for school administrators, focusing primarily on the needs of school principals. The site offers articles, profiles of principals, discussion boards, and a free weekly newsletter.

**HIGHLIGHTS FOR PRINCIPALS.** Topics for current and archived articles include funding, goals, leadership, programs, staffing, teacher training, and technology. Most articles are brief enough to read online and often include links to additional information. You can also print and read them offline. The discussion boards offer opportunities for you to post questions and comments.

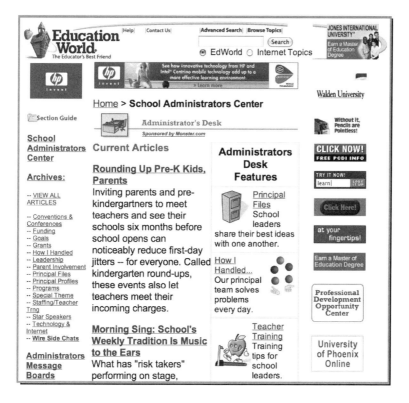

## TeAch-nology

www.teach-nology.com/edleadership/

**SITE DESCRIPTION.** TeAch-nology is a portal that provides access to hundreds of Web sites through categorized lists. Thirty-two categories include such topics as **Ability Grouping**, **Burnout and Stress Management**, **New to Management**, **Rural Education**, and **School Governance**.

**HIGHLIGHTS FOR PRINCIPALS.** To use the portal, click on a category that interests you. You'll then see a list of subcategories as well as annotated lists of links to Web sites that fit the general category. Narrow your search further by clicking on a subcategory, or scroll through the list and click on links.

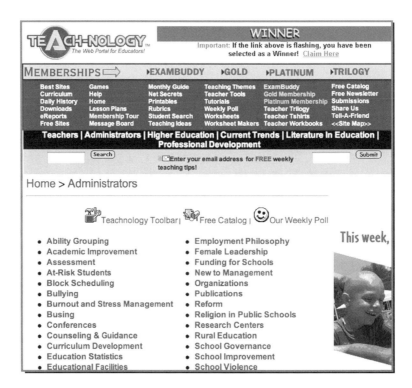

## U.S. Department of Education

**www.ed.gov**

**SITE DESCRIPTION.** The mission of the U.S. Department of Education is "to ensure equal access to education and to promote educational excellence for all Americans." Information about federal education initiatives is provided in the five areas listed on the right-hand side of the page:

- Grants & Contracts

- Financial Aid

- Research & Statistics

- Policy

- Programs

You can also scroll through the home page and select topics, click on links at the top of the home page, or use the search engine to access hundreds of publications. If the site displays a portal screen, click on the link for the **U.S. Department of Education** Web site.

**HIGHLIGHTS FOR PRINCIPALS.** In addition to the formal reports, articles, and other publications available here are excellent booklets designed for use with parents. Some documents may be downloaded, and others are available through the online ordering system. Many are free, but some are available for a small fee.

Be sure to click on the **Administrators** link at the top of the Home page. This takes you to a page that highlights information available throughout the site that will be of particular interest to school principals. Topics range from instructional leadership to funding information.

# Instruction

**W**hile an entire directory could be devoted to the topic of instruction, the Web sites in this section provide a broad range of information as quickly and easily as possible.

All address some aspect of classroom instruction, ranging from descriptions of common instructional strategies to models and lesson planning. Two sites are actually online lesson builders intended for student use, but they are effective in planning professional development workshops for adults as well. Several of the sites feature quick descriptions you can print and review with teachers in individual conferences or at staff meetings.

You may also want to visit the Association for Supervision and Curriculum Development (ASCD) at **www.ascd.org**, which is listed in the Professional Organizations section of this directory.

# QUICK REFERENCE CHART

| NAME OF SITE/INTERNET ADDRESS | PRIMARY AREA OF EMPHASIS | | | |
| --- | --- | --- | --- | --- |
| | LEARNING STYLES | LESSON DEVELOPMENT | MODELS | SUPERVISION |
| About Learning www.funderstanding.com/about_learning.cfm | ▓ | | | |
| Big6 big6.com | | | ▓ | |
| Block Scheduling education.umn.edu/carei/blockscheduling/ | | | ▓ | |
| Filamentality www.kn.sbc.com/wired/fil/ | | ▓ | ▓ | |
| Introduction to Teaching Strategies www.aea267.k12.ia.us/cia/framework/ strategies/ | | | ▓ | |
| Landmarks for Schools landmark-project.com | | ▓ | ▓ | |
| Leadership by Walking Around: Walkthroughs and Instructional Improvement www.principalspartnership.com/ feature203.html | | | ▓ | ▓ |
| NCRTEC Lesson Planner www.ncrtec.org/tl/lp/ | | ▓ | | |
| School Libraries & You: Administrators & School Board Members www.ala.org/ala/aasl/schlibrariesandyou/ administrators/schoollibraries.htm | | | ▓ | ▓ |

## About Learning

**www.funderstanding.com/about_learning.cfm**

**SITE DESCRIPTION.** This page provides brief overviews of 12 different theories about learning. Each overview includes a definition of the learning theory, a short discussion about the theory, an explanation of how this impacts learning, and at least one recommended reading.

**HIGHLIGHTS FOR PRINCIPALS.** We all covered this material in methods courses, but it's helpful to brush up on the concepts, particularly when teachers are putting the theory into practice. These short overviews on theories include **Constructivism**, **Piaget's Developmental Theory**, **Multiple Intelligences**, and nine others. Without being overwhelming, these summaries provide enough information to get your staff thinking about how children learn.

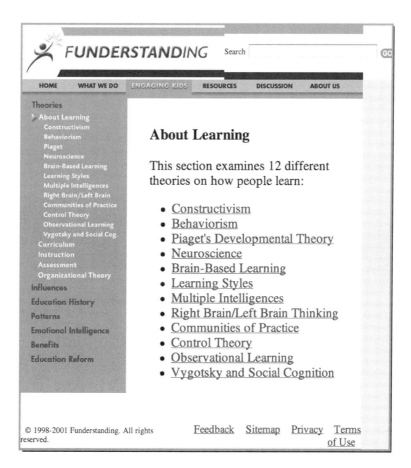

## Big6

### big6.com

**SITE DESCRIPTION.** Mike Eisenberg and Bob Berkowitz, leaders in promoting the concept of "information literacy," maintain this site. Areas of specific interest to principals include:

- **Overview:** The Big6 and Super3 approaches and how they can be used to teach information and technology skills

- **Lessons:** Sample lessons for Grades K–12 that can be used as models for teachers

- **Links:** Examples of information literacy projects across the country

- **Research:** Links to articles and reports about information literacy

- **Resources:** Tools you may use in implementing a Big6 or Super3 information literacy program

Also included is information about workshops, plus an online store where you can purchase Big6 materials for training and implementation.

**HIGHLIGHTS FOR PRINCIPALS.** Advances in technology, the focus on literacy of all kinds, and the trend to redefine the role of the library/media center in schools make it imperative that principals be up-to-date with this field. Visiting this site is an excellent starting point. Whether you need a basic understanding of the trends in information literacy or just want to keep your finger on the pulse of what's happening, this site is a valuable resource.

## Block Scheduling

education.umn.edu/carei/blockscheduling/

**SITE DESCRIPTION.** The Center for Applied Research and Educational Improvement (CAREI) at the University of Minnesota hosts this site on block scheduling. Four main areas include:

- **Primer & FAQ:** Frequently asked questions about block scheduling, including how to successfully implement it, professional development needed, and instructional strategies that work

- **Schools:** Lists of U.S. and international schools using block scheduling. Some are linked to the school's Web site

- **Discussion:** An e-mail list focused on information about block scheduling

- **Research and Resources:** Links to research about block scheduling (both positive and negative) and to other block-scheduling Web sites

**HIGHLIGHTS FOR PRINCIPALS.** This is a good resource if you're exploring the possibility of block scheduling at your site. The **Research and Resources** section is especially helpful, with links to information about block scheduling for various grade levels, for different settings (for example, rural schools), and for different student populations (such as special education). Sample block schedules are also provided.

If you already have block scheduling, you'll find useful the links to other schools and the e-mail list. Through these resources, you can communicate with other educators, find out what's working, or ask for advice and ideas.

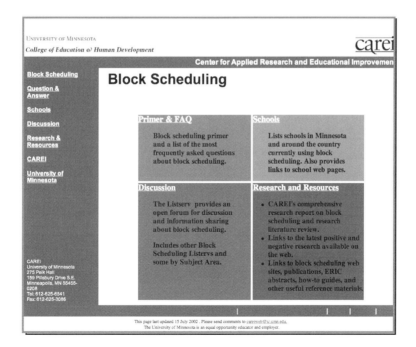

## Filamentality

**www.kn.sbc.com/wired/fil/**

**SITE DESCRIPTION.** According to the site description, "Filamentality is a fill-in-the-blank tool that guides you through picking a topic, searching the Web, gathering good Internet links, and turning them into learning activities." The end result is a Web-based activity you can share with others, such as hotlists of sites for students to visit or WebQuests, where students work in teams to solve a problem. The site is sponsored by SBC Knowledge Ventures.

**HIGHLIGHTS FOR PRINCIPALS.** Teachers appreciate resources they can use to find existing Web-based curricula or to teach them to easily develop their own. Use this site as a resource when helping teachers expand their use of technology in the curriculum. You can also use this site yourself to create Web-based activities for adults. For example, when working with technology planning teams, prepare a hotlist of sites the teams can use throughout the planning process.

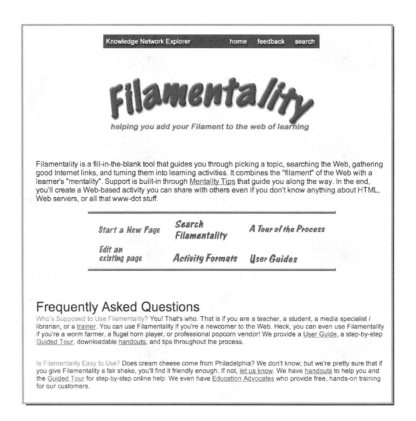

## Introduction to Teaching Strategies

www.aea267.k12.ia.us/cia/framework/strategies/

**SITE DESCRIPTION.** Sponsored by Area Education Agency 7 of Cedar Falls, Iowa, this site provides brief overviews of more than 30 different teaching strategies. Teachers and administrators may download a PDF file for each strategy. The file includes an overview about how to use the strategy and an example. (If you're not familiar with PDF files, refer to the Personal Productivity section of this directory to learn about Adobe Reader, a free program you can download to read PDF files.)

**HIGHLIGHTS FOR PRINCIPALS.** It's good to have access to a resource that can be used to broaden your thinking about ways to approach classroom instruction. These brief overviews will help you explore instructional alternatives. Educators are welcome to use the information to improve the quality of instruction in their schools.

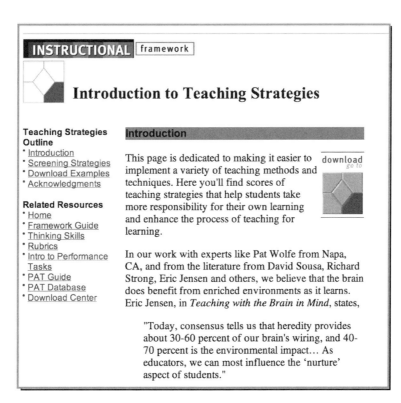

## Landmarks for Schools

### landmark-project.com

**SITE DESCRIPTION.** One of the earliest Web sites dedicated to education, Landmarks for Schools is an excellent resource for teachers interested in redefining the literacy skills their students need for the 21st century. It offers help in retooling classroom instruction to better prepare students. The site provides links to educational resources and easy-to-use Web tools.

**HIGHLIGHTS FOR PRINCIPALS.** As teachers explore ways to develop and deliver information-driven technology-supported instruction, they need tools to guide them through the process. Landmarks for Schools can offer this kind of support. Encourage teachers to review the links available here, particularly the **SLATE** page (the link is at the top of the page). SLATE stands for Strategic Learning and Teaching Environment. It helps teachers construct Web pages, including selecting appropriate links, providing a student workspace, and designing an assessment rubric. SLATE's **Rubric Builder** is very helpful for teachers learning how to create this kind of assessment instrument.

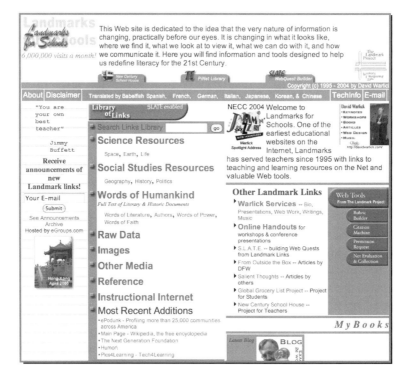

## Leadership by Walking Around:
## Walkthroughs and Instructional Improvement
www.principalspartnership.com/feature203.html

**SITE DESCRIPTION.** This link takes you to a featured article hosted by the Principals' Partnership Web site, a project sponsored by Union Pacific. Informal walkthrough classroom observations aren't a new concept, but have seen a surge in popularity recently. This article provides an overview of the practice and links to resources.

**HIGHLIGHTS FOR PRINCIPALS.** New principals will appreciate the step-by-step process for planning and implementing walkthrough observations. All administrators will find value in the links provided which offer additional reading, as well as tools administrators can use during walkthroughs.

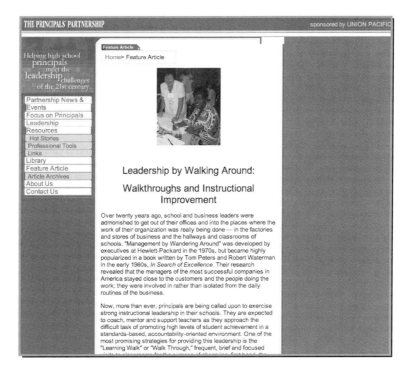

## NCRTEC Lesson Planner

www.ncrtec.org/tl/lp/

**SITE DESCRIPTION.** This site provides an online template for teachers to use when writing standards-based lesson plans. The site does not house plans, so users need to save or print their work before leaving the site. Directions for doing this are provided.

**HIGHLIGHTS FOR PRINCIPALS.** This tool serves two purposes. Teachers in the early stages of computer use who are looking for ways technology can make their lives a bit easier will appreciate the easy-to-use template. Teachers who need help writing more focused lesson plans are guided through each section of the plan by answering a series of specific questions.

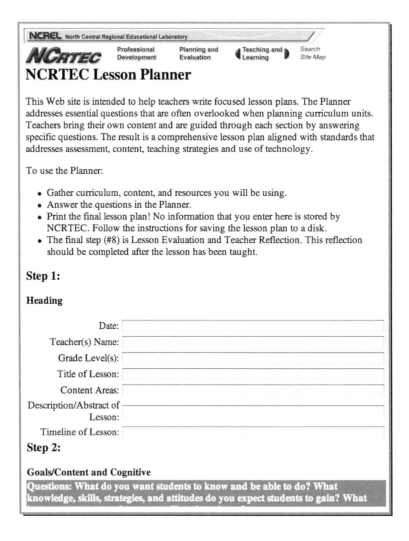

## School Libraries & You: Administrators & School Board Members

www.ala.org/ala/aasl/schlibrariesandyou/administrators/schoollibraries.htm

**SITE DESCRIPTION.** This page, hosted by the American Association for School Librarians (AASL), highlights information administrators need to know about school library programs. In times when budgets are tight, it's important that school leaders understand the critical role a strong library program can play in boosting student achievement.

**HIGHLIGHTS FOR PRINCIPALS.** Be sure to check out the brochure *Principal's Manual for Your School Library Media Program.* This downloadable guide for evaluating and planning school library media programs is targeted at principals in elementary and middle schools. The AASL Resource Guides are also worth reviewing. (Some resources are in PDF format. If you're not familiar with PDF files, refer to the Personal Productivity section of this directory to learn about Adobe Reader, a free program you can download to read PDF files.)

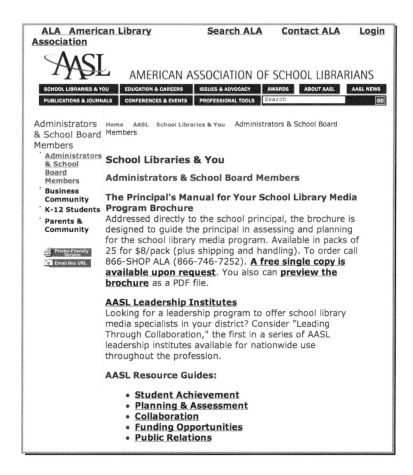

# Personal Productivity

**W**hile you don't want to become your own secretary, it's a good idea to sharpen your skills in the use of basic software programs and learn about tools that can streamline your technology use both online and offline. The Web sites listed in this section include tutorials for using Microsoft Office and other programs, a matrix that compares various Internet search engines, software programs that enable you to download and read PDF files as well as create your own, and an Internet-based tool for storing your own bookmarks for Internet sites.

# QUICK REFERENCE CHART

| NAME OF SITE/INTERNET ADDRESS | PRIMARY AREA OF EMPHASIS | | | |
| --- | --- | --- | --- | --- |
| | TUTORIAL | | UTILITY | |
| | INTERNET SKILLS | SOFTWARE APPLICATIONS | FILE MANAGEMENT | MANAGING BOOKMARKS |
| Adobe Reader www.adobe.com/products/acrobat/ readermain.html | | | software download | |
| Backflip www.backflip.com | | | | Internet-based |
| In and Out of the Classroom www.microsoft.com/education/ ?ID=IOCTutorials | download files for offline use | download files for offline use | | |
| Internet Search Tools Quick Reference Guide www.itrc.ucf.edu/conferences/pres/ srchtool.html | download matrix file | | | |
| Pdf995 www.pdf995.com/suite.html | | | software download | |

## Adobe Reader

**www.adobe.com/products/acrobat/readermain.html**

**SITE DESCRIPTION.** From this site, you can download and install a free copy of Adobe Reader. This software enables you to read and print files that are in PDF format. Under **Downloads** on the left-hand side of the page, click on **Free Adobe Reader**.

**HIGHLIGHTS FOR PRINCIPALS.** These days it's common to find that files accessible through Web pages are stored in PDF format. To access and use the files, you simply download a free copy of Adobe Reader. Sites often include a direct link to the Adobe download page. In that case, click on the link (often an Adobe icon) and follow the download directions. You can also go directly to the Adobe site to download the program. Once it's installed, you're all set to go when you encounter PDF files in your Web surfing.

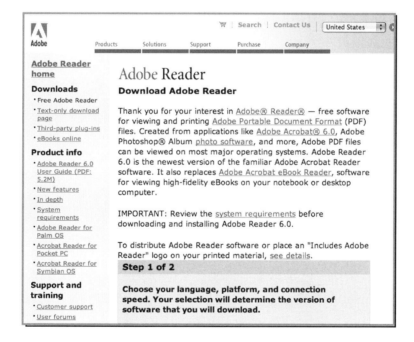

## Backflip

**www.backflip.com**

**SITE DESCRIPTION.** Backflip is a free service to bookmark and organize Web sites you'd like to visit again. You register for an account, then follow the simple directions to get started.

**HIGHLIGHTS FOR PRINCIPALS.** Have you had the experience of finding a site you really like, only to try to return later and not be able to find it? Or have you bookmarked a site at school and then not been able to access it from home? If you use just one computer system, the bookmarks in your browser are sufficient, once you know how to use them. But if you use more than one computer (such as at school and at home), browser-based bookmarks are limited because they're stored on the system you're using at the time you set the bookmark. Backflip, however, is Internet-based. When you bookmark a site using your Backflip account, you can access it later from any Internet-connected computer system by logging on to your account. You can also create a list—or folder—of sites and e-mail it to colleagues.

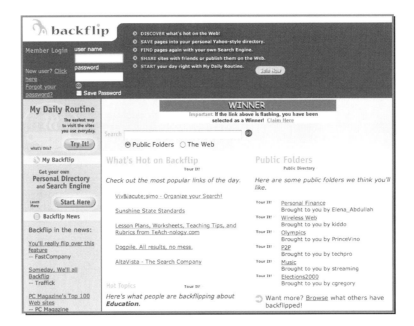

## In and Out of the Classroom

www.microsoft.com/education/?ID=IOCTutorials

**SITE DESCRIPTION.** Microsoft offers free tutorials to educators who want to learn to use various programs in a school setting. The files may be downloaded and used for staff development purposes. Current titles include:

- Office XP, Office 2001 and v. X for the Mac, Office 2000

- Windows NT 4.0, Windows 98

- FrontPage 2000

- Publisher 2000

- Managing E-Mail

- Excel 97

- PowerPoint 97

- Word 97

**HIGHLIGHTS FOR PRINCIPALS.** If you want to learn more about using a word processor, database, or spreadsheet for your own productivity, take a look at these tutorials. Designed for use by educators, the tutorials are self-paced and provide tips and tricks for making better use of the software. You may also share these files with staff.

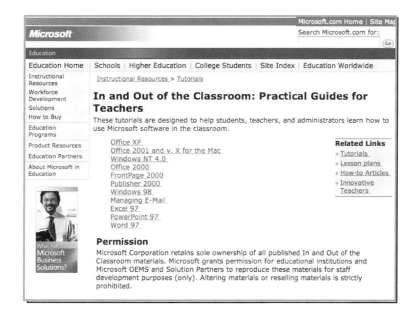

## Internet Search Tools Quick Reference Guide
www.itrc.ucf.edu/conferences/pres/srchtool.html

**SITE DESCRIPTION.** This page provides a matrix of commonly used search engines and Web portals. A second matrix offers tips and tricks for effective searching. The matrices are from the SouthEast Initiatives Regional Technology in Education Consortium (SEIR•TEC).

**HIGHLIGHTS FOR PRINCIPALS.** Ready to conduct your own searches online? This resource will help you design more productive searches by pointing out the strengths of various search engines and portals and what you can hope to find there. When accessing the matrices online, links take you directly to the various search engines and portals. You may also print them for offline reference.

### SEIR•TEC — Searching for help with technology integration?

The SouthEast Initiatives Regional Technology in Education Consortium (SEIR*TEC) promotes the use of technology to improve teaching and learning by providing technical assistance and authentic professional development in the areas of curriculum and instruction, leadership for technology, policy, planning and evaluation, with emphasis on benefiting traditionally underserved populations, such as low income, urban, rural, racial, and language minority populations. It is one of ten regional technology consortia funded by US Department of Education, and Office of Education Research and Improvement.

| Do you want to...? | ...Then try these tools! | | |
|---|---|---|---|
| Browse a broad topic? | Yahoo www.yahoo.com/ | What You Need to Know About www.miningco.com/ | Open Directory Project dmoz.org/ |
| Search for a narrow topic? | Google www.google.com/ | AltaVista www.altavista.com/ | All theWeb www.alltheweb.com/ |
| Search largest amount of Internet? (meta-search engines) | Ask Jeeves www.askjeeves.com/ | Dogpile www.dogpile.com/ | Vivisimo www.vivisimo.com/ |
| Browse educational topics and resources? | Schrock's Guide school.discovery.com /schrockguide/ | Education World www.education-world.com/ | Blue Web'n www.kn.pacbell.com/ wired/bluewebn/ |
| Search specific types of databases? | Switchboard (people) www.switchboard.com/ | MapQuest (places) www.mapquest.com/ | iTools www.iTools.com/ |
| Search for educational materials and reviews? | EvaluTech www.evalutech.sreb.org/ | FREE www.ed.gov/free/ | Gateway to Educational Materials (GEM) www.geminfo.org/ |
| Browse sites for students | Yahooligans www.yahooligans.com/ | Kids Click www.kidsclick.org/ | Sites en Espanol www.kn.pacbell.com/wired/fil/pages/listspanish.html |

**Who are the SEIR*TEC Partners?**
- SERVE
- Learning Innovations at WestEd (LI)
- National Center on Adult Literacy (NCAL) at University of Pennsylvania
- Southern Regional Education Board (SREB)
- Florida Instructional Technology Resource Center (ITRC) at the University of Central Florida

**Who does SEIR*TEC serve?**
- K-12 schools; teachers and communities; state education agencies; and preservice educators
- Alabama, Florida, Georgia, Mississippi, North Carolina, and South Carolina

**What does SEIR*TEC provide?**
- Curriculum-based Technology Initiatives
- Resources and Referrals
- Promising Practices
- Technical Assistance
- Professional Development
- Policy Briefs
- Support for Collaborative Initiatives
- Research and Dissemination

## Pdf995

www.pdf995.com/suite.html

**SITE DESCRIPTION.** This free software suite allows you to create your own files in PDF format. This is particularly useful for posting documents to your school Web site or when you are required to submit online grant proposals or reports.

**HIGHLIGHTS FOR PRINCIPALS.** Pdf995 is a great alternative for principals who need to create PDF files but can't afford to purchase a full version of Adobe Reader. Although a free PDF converter lacks some of the features of Adobe Reader, it's sufficient for most site administrators' needs. The suite consists of three separate downloads, so you can pick and choose the programs you need.

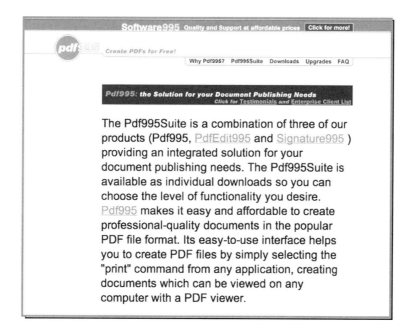

# Professional Development

**P**rofessional development for both teachers and administrators is a critical piece in improving student academic performance. However, even as the pressure increases for test scores to rise, the amount of time and funding provided for educators' professional growth seems to dwindle. The challenge for today's principal is to find a way to provide and attend training within the confines established by federal and state regulations and district policies, as well as certificated and classified staff contracts.

The following Web sites provide both administrators and teachers with information about training. Online training options are becoming increasingly prevalent, and one site takes you to a series of free online workshops. This may serve to introduce you and your staff to Internet-based instruction for adults. Two sites listed in the Professional Organizations section of this directory may also be helpful in answering your professional-growth needs. They are the Association for Supervision and Curriculum Development (ASCD) at **www.ascd.org** and the National Staff Development Council (NSDC) at **www.nsdc.org**.

# QUICK REFERENCE CHART

| NAME OF SITE/INTERNET ADDRESS | PRIMARY AREA OF EMPHASIS | | |
|---|---|---|---|
| | POLICY | PLANNING | RESOURCES |
| Career-Long Teacher Development: Policies That Make Sense **www.wested.org/cs/we/view/rs/469** | ■ | ■ | |
| Concept to Classroom: A Series of Workshops **www.thirteen.org/edonline/concept2class** | | | ■ |
| Edutopia Online: Professional Development **www.glef.org** | | | ■ |
| Financing Professional Development in Education **www.financeprojectinfo.org/ProfDevelop/Wallace.asp** | ■ | | |
| Linking Staff Development to Student Learning **www.mcrel.org/toolkit/process/ex-prof.asp** | | ■ | |
| Professional Development: Learning From the Best **www.ncrel.org/pd/toolkit.htm** | | ■ | |

## Career-Long Teacher Development: Policies That Make Sense

www.wested.org/cs/we/view/rs/469

**SITE DESCRIPTION.** This link takes you directly to a page where you can download a free PDF file of the policy brief *Career-Long Teacher Development: Policies That Make Sense*. You can order print copies at $8 each. (If you're not familiar with PDF files, refer to the Personal Productivity section of this directory to learn about Adobe Reader, a free program you can download to read PDF files.)

**HIGHLIGHTS FOR PRINCIPALS.** The brief is based on the work of Linda Darling-Hammond, professor of education at Stanford University. Ample research shows that the most important factor in student learning is the quality of the classroom teacher. Darling-Hammond argues that the best approach to ensuring the availability of highly qualified teachers is to transform and extend both teacher preparation and professional development activities so that teachers are supported in their own learning throughout their careers, starting with their recruitment into a teacher certification program. The brief is an excellent source of information on research and provides concrete suggestions for improving professional development practices.

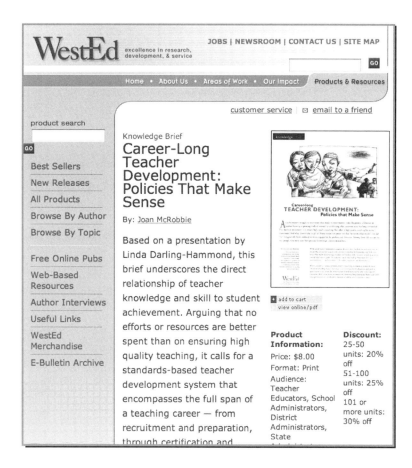

## Concept to Classroom: A Series of Workshops

www.thirteen.org/edonline/concept2class

**SITE DESCRIPTION.** This site offers free online professional development workshops designed by Thirteen Ed Online (Thirteen/WNET New York) in alliance with the Disney Learning Partnership. The 11 workshops cover a variety of topics, including **Tapping into Multiple Intelligences** and **Teaching to Academic Standards**. The workshops have been developed and reviewed by educational experts across the country. Each workshop takes between 30 and 35 hours to complete.

**HIGHLIGHTS FOR PRINCIPALS.** You can take advantage of the material offered here in a number of ways. Individual teachers who need to earn professional-growth hours can select and complete a workshop. Grade-level teachers may wish to work through a module as a study team, or you can conduct a workshop, such as **Teaching to Academic Standards**, for your entire staff. Workshops include reading, audio interviews, discussion topics, activities, and more.

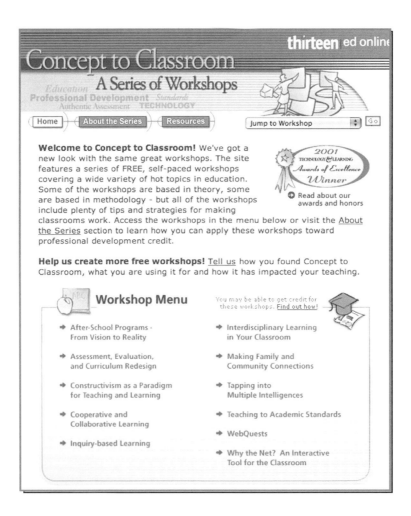

## Edutopia Online: Professional Development

www.glef.org

**SITE DESCRIPTION.** The George Lucas Foundation sponsors this site, which is used to document and disseminate models of innovative practices in K–12 schools. In addition to online professional development modules, the site offers free video clips and case studies.

**HIGHLIGHTS FOR PRINCIPALS.** The Professional Development area (click the **Professional Dev.** tab) includes eight free modules. Two focus on educational leadership and six address innovative classrooms. Each module contains articles, video clips, Power-Point presentations, and activities. Check out the modules for school leaders: **View of the Principal and the Job** and **Teacher Supervision & Development**. Also, take advantage of a free subscription to *Edutopia* magazine.

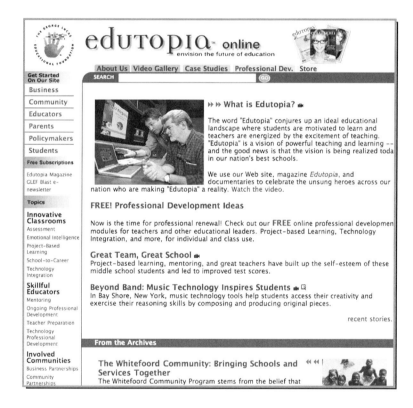

## Financing Professional Development in Education
www.financeprojectinfo.org/ProfDevelop/Wallace.asp

**SITE DESCRIPTION.** This site is the result of a partnership between Stanford University and The Finance Project. Using funding from the Wallace Foundation, the project is studying professional development for principals. The end result will be a report focused on the characteristics and components of high-quality professional development and how best to structure and finance these programs. In the meantime, the site provides links to many online resources and articles about all facets of professional development for educators.

**HIGHLIGHTS FOR PRINCIPALS.** Looking for information about the cost of professional development, how federal and state policies impact training, or the design and impact of professional development for teachers and administrators? Use the topic links provided on the home page to find a wide variety of useful resources. Many links are listed in each area, so you'll probably need to visit topics more than once to find all the gems here.

## Linking Staff Development to Student Learning

www.mcrel.org/toolkit/process/ex-prof.asp

**SITE DESCRIPTION.** This document is part of a larger report titled *Asking the Right Questions: A School Change Toolkit,* which looks at school reform. This page offers three steps to help staff focus on professional development needs through the use of guiding questions you can develop specifically for your site. The chart provided is particularly helpful.

**HIGHLIGHTS FOR PRINCIPALS.** It's easy to say that professional development should be directly tied to student learning, but this is often more difficult to actually plan and implement. Use this document with your staff as a tool for developing guiding questions that will help you focus on, and meet the needs of, both students and the teaching staff. Examples and suggested action steps are included.

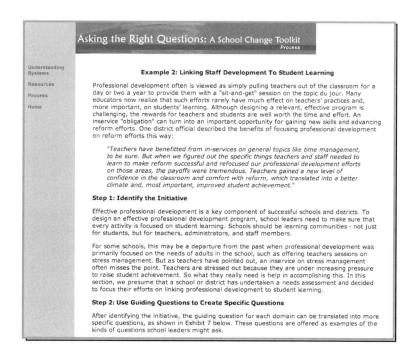

## Professional Development: Learning From the Best

**www.ncrel.org/pd/toolkit.htm**

**SITE DESCRIPTION.** This free toolkit for planning and implementing a professional development program is available through the North Central Regional Educational Laboratory (NCREL). The toolkit was developed using award-winning professional development programs as a foundation. You can download the toolkit in PDF format or order a no-cost print version at this site. (If you're not familiar with PDF files, refer to the Personal Productivity section of this directory to learn about Adobe Reader, a free program you can download to read PDF files.)

**HIGHLIGHTS FOR PRINCIPALS.** With the continued demand for school reform and accountability, coupled with decreased time for professional development of any kind, it's more critical than ever that training opportunities be well planned and effective. This toolkit is a good resource for you and your staff as you work to establish an effective professional development program. Topics include:

- Involving Others
- Setting Goals
- Needs Assessment
- Funding
- Finding Time
- Evaluating

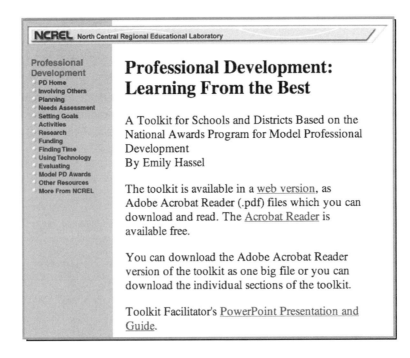

# Professional Organizations

Affiliation with professional organizations at local, state, and national levels is a way for principals, assistant principals, and other site administrators to stay in touch with one another and keep up with trends in the field. The organizations listed here are either specifically for district-level administrators or offer important information for school-site administrators. Though national, many support affiliates or special interest groups at the state and local level.

Each group listed offers professional development opportunities for its members, and most attempt to respond to general areas of concern for site administrators. The Quick Reference Chart identifies each group's primary areas of emphasis based on the stated mission or goals of the group.

# QUICK REFERENCE CHART

| NAME OF SITE/INTERNET ADDRESS | PRIMARY AREA OF EMPHASIS | | | | |
|---|---|---|---|---|---|
| | TARGET AUDIENCE | CURRICULUM | SUPERVISION | TECHNOLOGY | ADVOCACY |
| American Association of School Administrators (AASA) www.aasa.org | district/site administrators | | | | ▓ |
| Association for Supervision and Curriculum Development (ASCD) www.ascd.org | education leaders | ▓ | ▓ | | |
| International Society for Technology in Education (ISTE) www.iste.org | education leaders | ▓ | | ▓ | |
| National Association of Elementary School Principals (NAESP) www.naesp.org | site administration | | | | ▓ |
| National Association of Secondary School Principals (NASSP) www.nassp.org | site administration | ▓ | ▓ | | |
| National Middle School Association (NMSA) www.nmsa.org | education leaders | ▓ | | | |
| National Staff Development Council (NSDC) www.nsdc.org | education leaders | | ▓ | | |

# American Association of School Administrators

**www.aasa.org**

**ORGANIZATION DESCRIPTION.** Founded in 1865, the American Association of School Administrators (AASA) offers support to elementary and secondary school district administrators.

**BENEFITS OF MEMBERSHIP.** Access to AASA's online Network Program; special interest groups for AASA members; subscription to *The School Administrator;* reduced rates for conferences and other events; advocacy activities; discounts on books and other materials; legal-support program.

**SITE DESCRIPTION.** Much of the information is geared toward district-level administrators; however, site-level administrators will find helpful material in:

- **Links:** Access to Internet sites and reports in 11 categories, which currently include **News**, **Reports & Resources**, **Government**, and **In the Classroom**

- **Issues and Insights:** Reports, articles, and Internet resources, including **School Configuration & Scheduling**, **Assessment/Standards**, **Grants & Funding**, **Safe Schools**, **Data-driven Decision Making**, **Technology**, and more

**HIGHLIGHTS FOR PRINCIPALS.** Visit the **News** category in the **Links** area to access several daily headlines news services. Check out the online version of *The School Administrator.* Many of the articles are germane to site administrators. Save research time by taking advantage of the wealth of information available through the **Issues and Insights** area.

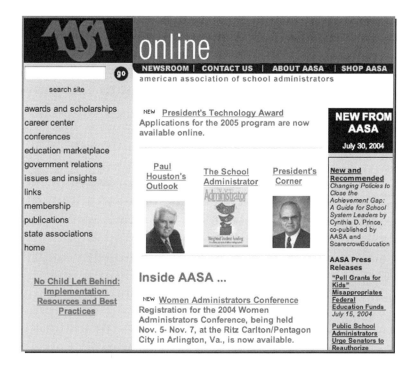

## Association for Supervision and Curriculum Development

www.ascd.org

**ORGANIZATION DESCRIPTION.** An international organization, the Association for Supervision and Curriculum Development (ASCD) is focused on issues concerning staff development and curriculum. Membership is open to educators in all positions, school board members, parents, and students.

**BENEFITS OF MEMBERSHIP.** Three types of membership offer increasing levels of service. All members receive eight issues of *Educational Leadership* magazine annually, along with two newsletters, discounts on products and conferences, and access to members-only areas of the Web site. For additional fees, ASCD also offers membership in affiliates and networks.

**SITE DESCRIPTION.** The two primary areas of interest for site administrators are:

- **News & Issues:** Education Issues, Policy News, and Policy Publications
- **Education Topics:** Excerpts from books and articles related to topics such as Classroom Management, Mentoring, and Standards

**HIGHLIGHTS FOR PRINCIPALS.** ASCD's publications are excellent resources. Visit the **Education Topics** area to access book excerpts and online articles from the journals. Sign up for a free subscription to the online *Research Brief* or *EDPolicy Update* e-newsletters, available in the **Publications** area.

# International Society for Technology in Education

**www.iste.org**

**ORGANIZATION DESCRIPTION.** The International Society for Technology in Education (ISTE) is a nonprofit professional organization with membership representing instructional technology leaders around the world. ISTE promotes appropriate use of technology to support teaching, learning, and administration in K–12 education and teacher education.

**BENEFITS OF MEMBERSHIP.** A subscription to the online newsletter *ISTE Update* and either *Learning & Leading with Technology* (eight issues annually) or *Journal of Research on Technology in Education* (four issues annually); free membership in one special interest group; 10% discount on ISTE books; conferences, workshops, and other professional development opportunities; and national advocacy activities.

**SITE DESCRIPTION.** Five areas of interest to administrators are:

- **L&L:** Current and back issues of *Learning & Leading with Technology* magazine. Some articles may be read online; others may be downloaded by members.

- **NETS:** The National Educational Technology Standards, developed for students, teachers, and administrators. Includes support materials.

- **Professional Development:** Conferences, workshops, and symposia.

- **Educator Resources:** Listings of current books, Web sites, and periodicals on technology in education.

- **Research Projects:** White papers, studies, and reports.

**HIGHLIGHTS FOR PRINCIPALS.** Visit the **NETS** area, an extensive resource on technology standards for students, teachers, and administrators. This area includes standards, performance indicators, and support material such as profiles and lesson plans. For supporting documentation, visit the **Research Projects** area, particularly the **Center for Applied Research in Educational Technology** (CARET) and the **Reports** sections.

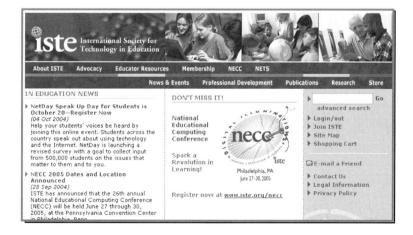

## National Association of Elementary School Principals

**www.naesp.org**

**ORGANIZATION DESCRIPTION.** The mission of the National Association of Elementary School Principals (NAESP) is to be a leader in advocacy and support for elementary and middle school administrators and leaders.

**BENEFITS OF MEMBERSHIP.** Joining NAESP includes a subscription to *Principal,* a bimonthly journal, and several newsletters. Materials available through the National Principals Resource Center are discounted to members; so are registration fees for conferences and professional development opportunities.

**SITE DESCRIPTION.** In addition to information about membership, principals will find helpful materials in the following areas:

- **Education News:** Links to breaking education news from national publications

- **Career Center: Job Openings** and **Post Your Resume** forums

- **Professional Development:** Workshops, seminars, conferences, online academy

**HIGHLIGHTS FOR PRINCIPALS.** Check out the **Education News** links for quick updates on hot education topics. Need advice or ideas from fellow administrators? The **Education Network** and **International Leadership** forums (found under **Network**, then **Online Forums**) are there for you to post questions or read through discussions of various topics. Looking for current articles? Visit the **Publications** area to access samples from *Principal* and various newsletters.

# National Association of Secondary School Principals

**www.nassp.org**

**ORGANIZATION DESCRIPTION.** Since 1916, the National Association of Secondary School Principals (NASSP) has served as a professional organization for middle and high school principals, assistant principals, and aspiring principals.

**BENEFITS OF MEMBERSHIP.** Five levels of membership are offered: individual, institutional, educator, retired, and international. The most comprehensive levels include legal coverage in the form of liability protection, legal-fee reimbursement, and legal advice; subscriptions to periodicals and newsletters; reduced rates for conference and meeting fees; discounts on materials; and more.

**SITE DESCRIPTION.** The home page features timely articles from the *Bulletin* and *Principal Leadership*. Additional areas of interest include:

- **Professional Development:** Tools for assessment and development of individual administrators' skills, **Message Boards** with numerous Open Topics and Ask a Mentor

- **What's New**: Recently posted bulletins, reports, and other documents

- **Advocacy:** Government relations, public relations, and **Principal'ccs Legislative Action Center**

- **Publications:** Links to current articles from NASSP publications

- **School Improvement:** Information about **Safe & Orderly Schools**, literacy, special education, testing and assessment, and more.

**HIGHLIGHTS FOR PRINCIPALS.** Visit the **Developing Yourself** section of the **Professional Development** area, where you can assess your own skills and knowledge, then access documents designed to help you create an individual development plan and learn how to work with a mentor. Join a discussion group. Sign up for NASSP's free biweekly e-mail newsletter.

## National Middle School Association

**www.nmsa.org**

**ORGANIZATION DESCRIPTION.** The National Middle School Association (NMSA) has 30,000 members, including teachers, school administrators, community members, and university faculty.

**BENEFITS OF MEMBERSHIP.** Individual and student, parent, or retiree memberships offer one-year subscriptions to five publications; discounts on conferences, workshops, and publications; and eligibility to vote for NMSA officers. Institutional memberships provide four one-year subscriptions to each of five publications, eligibility to nominate and vote for NMSA officers, and discounts on conferences, workshops, and publications.

**SITE DESCRIPTION.** Access to a wealth of articles and professional development opportunities.

- **News & Views:** Articles, press releases, and reports
- **Month of the Young Adolescent:** An annual event that brings together a coalition of national organizations focused on the needs of children ages 10–15
- **Professional Development:** Information about conferences, workshops, online training, and video training
- **Services/Resources:** Curriculum ideas, publications, job connections, and more
- **Research:** Online reports, articles, and research summaries

**HIGHLIGHTS FOR PRINCIPALS.** Visit the **Principals Online** bulletin board (go to the **Professional Development** section, then to **Online Training** for the link). Here you can post questions, share ideas, or connect with fellow middle school administrators.

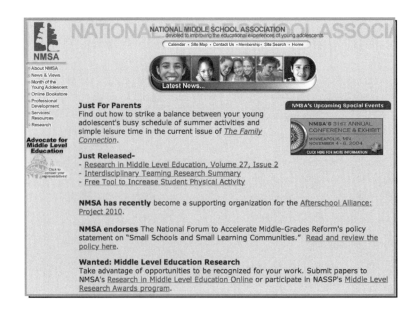

# National Staff Development Council

**www.nsdc.org**

**ORGANIZATION DESCRIPTION.** Founded in 1969, the National Staff Development Council (NSDC) is dedicated to school improvement through high-quality staff development programs.

**BENEFITS OF MEMBERSHIP.** There are three levels of membership. Individual members receive the *Journal of Staff Development* (quarterly), *NSDC Networking Guide,* and either *Results* (eight issues annually) or *Tools for Schools* (bimonthly newsletter). Comprehensive individual members receive all the above along with subscriptions to both newsletters and access to members-only areas of the Web site. Organizational members are entitled to all the above plus three vouchers to waive the nonmember conference fee.

**SITE DESCRIPTION.** These areas are of particular interest to school principals:

- **NSDC Standards:** Help for creating effective staff development programs
- **Staff Development Library:** Extensive collection of articles from NSDC publications

**HIGHLIGHTS FOR PRINCIPALS.** The NSDC standards for staff development can be used as a foundation for your professional development program. The **Staff Development FAQs** found under **Staff Development Basics** in the library can be used to provide information to teachers and parents. The library articles are indispensable for committees engaged in professional development planning.

# Professional Reading

I nternet-based publications are helpful for keeping up with trends and issues in education news. You can subscribe to e-newsletters that are sent to your e-mailbox or visit Web sites at any time. While these electronic publications don't replace print materials, they are useful for quick article searches or just a fast read.

# QUICK REFERENCE CHART

| NAME OF SITE/INTERNET ADDRESS | PRIMARY AREA OF EMPHASIS | | | | |
| --- | --- | --- | --- | --- | --- |
| | FREQUENCY OF PUBLICATION | | | FORMAT | |
| | DAILY | WEEKLY | OTHER | e-NEWS-LETTER | e-ZINE/JOURNAL |
| ASCD's SmartBrief<br>**www.smartbrief.com/ascd/** | ■ | | | ■ | |
| The Doyle Report<br>**www.thedoylereport.com** | | ■ | | ■ | |
| Ed Week Update<br>**www.edweek.org** | | ■ | | ■ | |
| eSchool News This Week<br>**www.eschoolnews.com/emailprofile/** | | ■ | | ■ | |
| PEN Weekly NewsBlast<br>**www.publiceducation.org** | | ■ | | ■ | |
| Phi Delta Kappan<br>**www.pdkintl.org/kappan/kappan.htm** | | | 10 issues | | ■ |
| Reading Online<br>**www.readingonline.org** | | | monthly | | ■ |
| Scholastic Administr@tor<br>**www.scholastic.com/administrator/** | | | quarterly | | ■ |
| School Administrator<br>**www.aasa.org/publications/sa/** | | | 11 issues | | ■ |
| Technology and Learning Magazine<br>**www.techlearning.com/content/about/<br>tl_current.html** | | | 11 issues | | ■ |
| Today's School<br>**www.peterli.com/ts/** | | | 9 issues | | ■ |

## ASCD's SmartBrief

**www.smartbrief.com/ascd/**

**RESOURCE DESCRIPTION.** This free e-newsletter is delivered to your e-mailbox Monday through Friday. Articles dealing with curriculum, professional leadership, technology solutions, policy, association news, and stories from the field are summarized, with links to the full text provided. These articles are culled from various national publications.

**HIGHLIGHTS FOR PRINCIPALS.** Simply skimming the SmartBrief digest keeps you up to speed on education headlines. When an article catches your eye, click on the link to read the full text. This is one of the best tools around for staying on top of trends and issues in education.

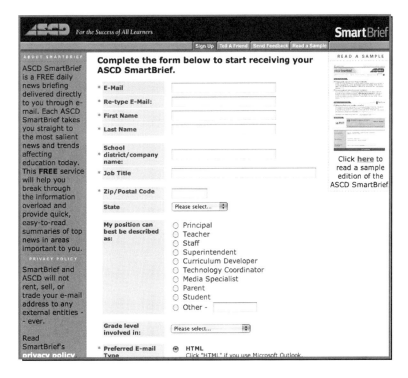

## The Doyle Report

**www.thedoylereport.com**

**RESOURCE DESCRIPTION.** This free weekly publication focuses on the intersection of school reform and technology in education. Included are editorials on hot topics, spotlight interviews with nationally known educators, technology in the news, reviews of important education events, information on federal initiatives, and more. Past reports are archived for easy retrieval.

**HIGHLIGHTS FOR PRINCIPALS.** Sign up for the report and it will be sent each week. It takes just a few minutes to skim the start of each article. Want more information? Click on the **Full story...** link to read the rest. A forum area is provided in case you'd like to post a question or comment about an article.

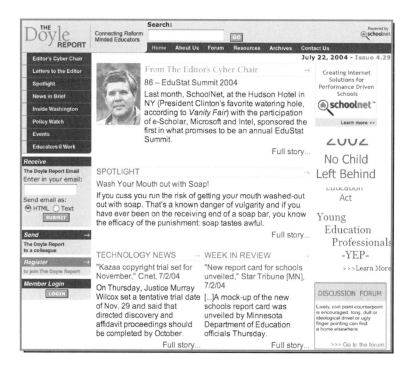

## Ed Week Update

**www.edweek.org**

**RESOURCE DESCRIPTION.** This free weekly e-mail digest highlights selected articles from the current issue of *Education Week,* as well as special reports and other stories of national interest. Besides visiting here to subscribe, additional information is available on the Education Week Web site.

**HIGHLIGHTS FOR PRINCIPALS.** The e-mail digest helps you focus on major stories and keep up with special reports. Each item is briefly described, and a link to the complete article takes you to the Education Week Web site to read the entire text. To subscribe, click on the **E-Newsletters** link on the home page and fill out the registration form.

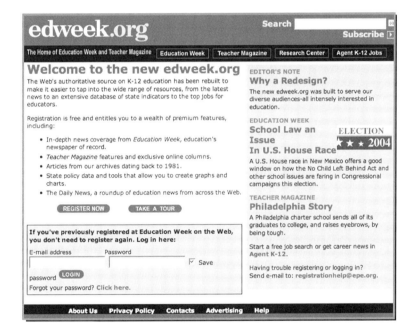

## eSchool News This Week

**www.eschoolnews.com/emailprofile/**

**RESOURCE DESCRIPTION.** *eSchool News This Week* is a free weekly e-newsletter focusing on breaking news in educational technology and how the use of technology affects schools. Topics include tech funding news; grants, awards, and deadlines; site of the week; and a comprehensive school technology events calendar.

**HIGHLIGHTS FOR PRINCIPALS.** This newsletter will help you keep up with the ever-changing landscape of educational technology. The funding section is especially helpful. All summaries include links back to the eSchool News site for complete information.

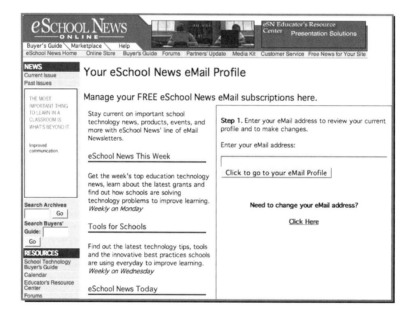

## PEN Weekly NewsBlast

### www.publiceducation.org

**RESOURCE DESCRIPTION.** Sponsored by the Public Education Network, *PEN Weekly NewsBlast* is a free e-newsletter with articles about school improvement as well as grant and funding information. The articles are gleaned from a variety of national publications. Each summary is linked to the full-text article. Sign up directly from the home page, or click on **NewsBlast** to view the current issue.

**HIGHLIGHTS FOR PRINCIPALS.** Articles emphasize a global approach to the school improvement movement. For example, recent articles included "State Implementation of the No Child Left Behind Act" and "Americans Seek Fairness In Public School Funding." The funding and grant information is also very helpful. Past issues are archived online.

### Phi Delta Kappan

www.pdkintl.org/kappan/kappan.htm

**RESOURCE DESCRIPTION.** The print version of *Phi Delta Kappan* has been published since 1915. While the online version doesn't replace the print journal, you'll find two to four articles from each issue available through the Web site.

**HIGHLIGHTS FOR PRINCIPALS.** Visit the **Articles Online** section to find material, listed by issue, from recent journals. If you're looking for a specific topic, use the **Research** area link at the top of the page. From there, you can request a free database search of articles back to 1970. Be sure you have a good idea what you're looking for so that you can supply keywords to assist in the search.

pdkintl home | site map |

## Phi Delta Kappan

**Articles  Research  Subscriptions  Submissions  Advertising**

*Phi Delta Kappan,* the professional print journal for education, addresses policy issues for educators at all levels. Advocating research-based school reform, the *Kappan* provides a forum for debate on controversial subjects. Published since 1915, the journal appears monthly September through June.

IN THIS ISSUE

TABLE OF CONTENTS
ARTICLES ONLINE
BACKTALK: E-MAIL THE EDITORS
ADVERTISERS

GALLUP POLL LINKS
JOBSITE

### Former *Kappan* Editor Stanley Elam Dies

On 14 November 2003, Stanley M. Elam, editor of the *Kappan* from 1956 through December 1980, passed away quietly at his Florida residence after a long illness. Elam was born in 1916 and grew up on a farm in central Illinois. He attended a rural elementary school and in 1934 was valedictorian of Stewardson District High School. It was there that he acquired the ambition to be a journalist.

## Reading Online

**www.readingonline.org**

**RESOURCE DESCRIPTION.** *Reading Online* is a journal about K–12 practice and research, published by the International Reading Association (IRA). The site includes:

- peer-reviewed articles
- ideas and information about using technology to support reading instruction
- international perspectives on teaching literacy
- discussions about information literacy
- online communities for networking

**HIGHLIGHTS FOR PRINCIPALS.** Student literacy is an important issue. K–12 principals need to understand changes in approaches to teaching literacy at all grade levels. This online journal can be used to keep up with trends in this important field. The articles on new literacies and the even emphasis across grade levels in the peer-reviewed articles make this a valuable resource for all principals.

## Scholastic Administr@tor

www.scholastic.com/administrator/

**RESOURCE DESCRIPTION.** *Scholastic Administr@tor* magazine, published by Scholastic, targets school administrators and education technology leaders. The feature articles and columns cover topics such as educational leadership, appropriate use of technology, student achievement, professional development, and funding. Free subscriptions to the print version are available to qualified educators.

**HIGHLIGHTS FOR PRINCIPALS.** This is a helpful resource when you need to deal with instructional technology issues. In addition to current articles, an archive is available. It's somewhat limited at this point because the publication is new, but it has promise. You may also be interested in the **Technology Standards Self-Assessment Survey**, accessible through the **Technology** tab. The assessment is based on the Technology Standards for School Administrators, now known as the National Educational Technology Standards for Administrators, or NETS•A.

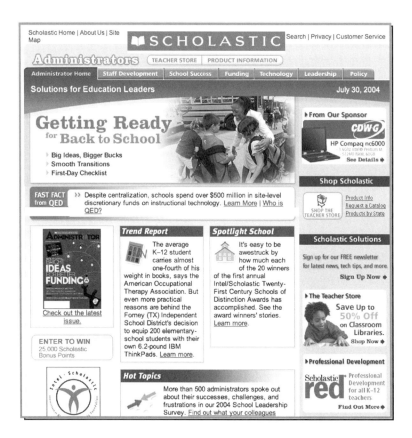

## School Administrator

**www.aasa.org/publications/sa/**

**RESOURCE DESCRIPTION.** This link takes you to the online version of *The School Administrator* magazine, published by the American Association of School Administrators. In addition to the current issue, you can access archives back to January 1997. The online magazine includes feature articles, guest columns, executive committee member columns, and profiles.

**HIGHLIGHTS FOR PRINCIPALS.** Although the publication targets school district administrators, principals will find that many of the articles relate to site issues. For example, several articles in a recent issue focused on "principal challenges."

## Technology and Learning Magazine

www.techlearning.com/content/about/tl_current.html

**RESOURCE DESCRIPTION.** *Technology and Learning Magazine* is a mainstay for educators interested in instructional technology. Appropriate technology use to support student and teacher learning is a theme the publication has supported since its inception. The online magazine features articles on professional development, technology integration, best practices, and more. The archive goes back to 1997. You may also sign up online for a free subscription to the print magazine.

**HIGHLIGHTS FOR PRINCIPALS.** The magazine's editors recognize the importance of the role of school administrators in implementing successful technology-enhanced programs. As you search the archives, you'll find a number of articles aimed at site administrators.

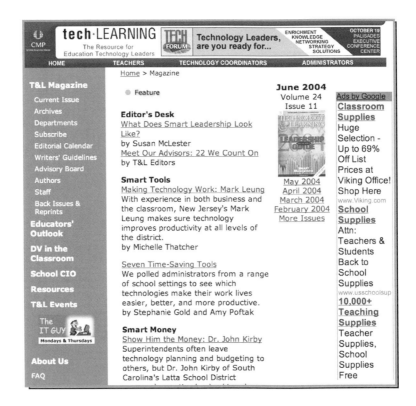

## Today's School

**www.peterli.com/ts/**

**RESOURCE DESCRIPTION.** Published by Peter Li Education Group, *Today's School* magazine targets administrators of site-based-managed schools. A free subscription to the print version may be requested on the site. You may also access feature articles, columns, and other material online.

**HIGHLIGHTS FOR PRINCIPALS.** The breadth of topics covered in this publication make it attractive to principals whether or not they are at a site-based-managed school. School solutions, technology, facilities, fund-raising, and curriculum issues are just some of the areas regularly addressed.

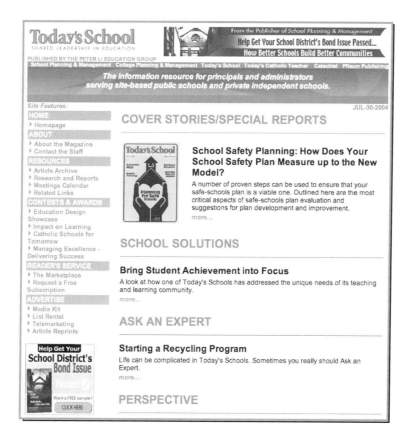

# Research Institutes and Education Centers

A term principals hear frequently these days is "research-based," particularly in conjunction with the No Child Left Behind Act. Where do you find the research you're to use when making decisions about programs? The U.S. Department of Education sponsors 10 Regional Education Laboratories (RELs) across the United States. Each REL provides services to designated clusters of states and is also assigned a specialty to research, develop materials for, and disseminate information on nationally. The RELs are located at nonprofit institutions that also work on other projects, so each is a potential gold mine for educators. At each Web site you'll find reports, briefs, toolkits, model lessons, and much more. Although you can access a page through the Institute of Education Sciences (IES) site that lists these RELs and is included in this section, this directory provides descriptions to help you identify the specific lab offering information you might require.

Links to three additional research sources are also provided.

# QUICK REFERENCE CHART

| NAME OF SITE/INTERNET ADDRESS | PRIMARY AREA OF EMPHASIS | |
| --- | --- | --- |
| | REGIONAL EDUCATION LABORATORY SPECIALTY AREA | OTHER ORGANIZATIONS' AREAS OF SPECIALTY |
| Annenberg Institute for School Reform www.annenberginstitute.org | | school reform |
| Appalachia Educational Laboratory (AEL) www.ael.org | unlocking today's technologies for tomorrow's students | |
| The Education Alliance at Brown University www.alliance.brown.edu | teaching diverse learners | |
| Institute of Education Sciences (IES) www.ed.gov/about/offices/list/ies/ index.html?src=mr | | national statistics, best practices |
| Laboratory for Student Success (LSS): The Mid-Atlantic Regional Educational Laboratory www.temple.edu/LSS/ | educational leadership | |
| Mid-continent Research for Education and Learning (McREL) www.mcrel.org | standards-based instructional practice | |
| North Central Regional Educational Laboratory (NCREL) www.ncrel.org | technology | |
| Northwest Regional Educational Laboratory (NWREL) www.nwrel.org | re-engineering schools for improvement | |
| Pacific Resources for Education and Learning (PREL) www.prel.org | curriculum and instruction on reading and language mastery | |
| RAND Education www.rand.org/education/ | | assessment and accountability, school reform evaluation |
| Southeast Regional Vision for Education (SERVE) www.serve.org | expanded learning opportunities | |
| Southwest Educational Development Laboratory (SEDL) www.sedl.org | family and community connections with schools | |
| WestEd www.wested.org | assessment of educational achievement | |

## The Education Alliance at Brown University

www.alliance.brown.edu

**SITE DESCRIPTION.** The Education Alliance at Brown University is home to the Northeast and Islands Regional Educational Laboratory, one of 10 regional laboratories across the country which serves New York, New England, the Virgin Islands, and Puerto Rico. In addition to the research and development work done, this lab focuses on secondary school redesign, professional learning, educational leadership, and providing field services to state and local education agencies within its service area. Two additional noteworthy projects found here are the New England Equity Assistance Center and the Knowledge Loom.

**HIGHLIGHTS FOR PRINCIPALS.** Visit the various topic areas to browse related publications. Many of the documents can be downloaded, and for several others, single print copies can be ordered at no cost. A number of publications in different areas address **Equity and Diversity**. Access information about the Knowledge Loom in the **Technology** area (select **Projects** from the list on the left).

## Institute of Education Sciences

**www.ed.gov/about/offices/list/ies/index.html?src=mr**

**SITE DESCRIPTION.** The Institute of Education Sciences (IES), formerly the Office of Educational Research and Improvement (OERI), is part of the U.S. Department of Education. It supports educational research, collects and analyzes educational statistics, identifies promising and exemplary instructional programs, and collects and disseminates material from a variety of sources. The results of these efforts are made available through five areas of the Web site:

- **Programs/Initiatives**
- **Reports & Resources**
- **Evaluation Center**
- **Research Center**
- **Statistics Center**

**HIGHLIGHTS FOR PRINCIPALS.** On November 5, 2002, the Education Sciences Reform Act of 2002 was signed into law, replacing OERI with IES, a new organization. The change reflects the intent of the president and Congress to advance the field of education research, mandating more rigorous research in support of evidence-based education. The new institute consists of three centers: the National Center for Education Evaluation and Regional Assistance (**Evaluation Center**), the National Center for Education Research (**Research Center**), and the National Center for Education Statistics (**Statistics Center**). Spend time browsing each center to find information related to research design and results.

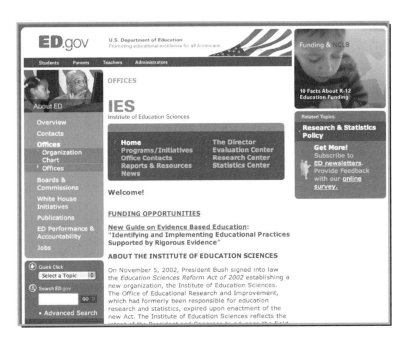

## Laboratory for Student Success:
## The Mid-Atlantic Regional Educational Laboratory

www.temple.edu/LSS/

**SITE DESCRIPTION.** One of 10 regional laboratories across the country, the Laboratory for Student Success (LSS) serves Delaware, Maryland, New Jersey, Pennsylvania, and Washington, D.C.; however, the information here is of value to principals throughout the nation. In addition to research and development, this lab takes the lead nationally in educational leadership, advanced technologies for learning, learning communities, comprehensive school reform, and field services to schools within its service area. It's sponsored by the Temple University Center for Research in Human Development and Education.

**HIGHLIGHTS FOR PRINCIPALS.** The **Publications** area includes findings from work done at this lab and other national R & D resources. Click on the **Publications Library** link to browse available materials. These publications are available online, but you can also order print copies. In addition, a number of books and videos can be purchased online. With its emphasis on educational leadership, you'll find many documents relating to the principal's role in education and reform.

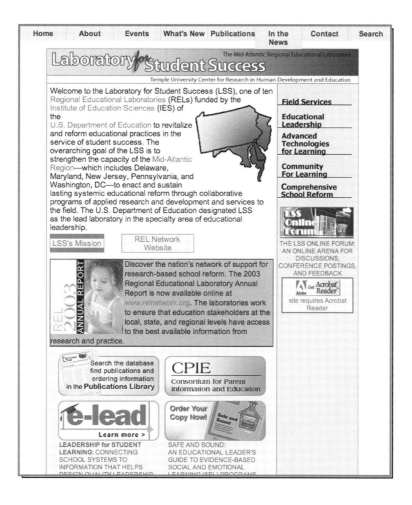

## Mid-continent Research for Education and Learning
### www.mcrel.org

**SITE DESCRIPTION.** One of 10 regional laboratories across the country, the Mid-continent Research for Education and Learning (McREL) serves Colorado, Kansas, Missouri, Nebraska, North Dakota, South Dakota, and Wyoming; however, the information here is of value to principals throughout the nation. In addition to the research and development work done, this lab operates the Mid-continent **Eisenhower Regional Consortium**, supports the Region IX Comprehensive Assistance Center, and provides field services to state and local education agencies within its service area.

**HIGHLIGHTS FOR PRINCIPALS.** One of the most valuable resources on this site is the searchable standards database for both K–12 academics and career-based education. Use the **McREL's Quick Links** menu to select **Compendium—K–12 Standards**. You may also want to browse the **Regional Educational Laboratory** area for resources tied directly to McREL projects.

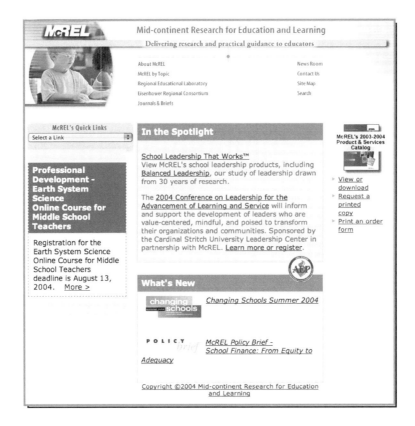

## North Central Regional Educational Laboratory

www.ncrel.org

**SITE DESCRIPTION.** One of 10 regional laboratories across the country, the North Central Regional Educational Laboratory (NCREL) serves Illinois, Indiana, Iowa, Michigan, Minnesota, Ohio, and Wisconsin; however, the information here is of value to principals throughout the nation. In addition to research and development, this lab specializes in educational applications of technology, operates the **North Central Eisenhower Mathematics and Science Consortium** and the **North Central Regional Technology in Education Consortium**, and provides field services to state and local education agencies within its service area.

**HIGHLIGHTS FOR PRINCIPALS.** Don't miss the **Pathways to School Improvement** area. This comprehensive resource brings research, policy, and classroom practice together into concise briefs invaluable to school principals. Current topics are **Assessment, At-Risk Students, Family & Community, Instruction, Leadership, Literacy, Mathematics & Science, Policy, Professional Development**, and **Technology in Education**. Additional topics can be accessed through the archives. You can also download or order materials through the **Product Catalog**, accessible through the Quick Links drop-down menu at the bottom of the page.

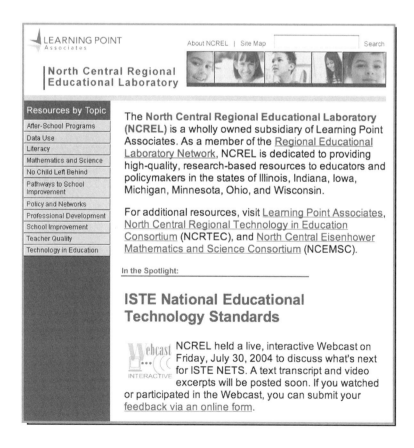

## Northwest Regional Educational Laboratory

**www.nwrel.org**

**SITE DESCRIPTION.** One of 10 regional laboratories across the country, the Northwest Regional Educational Laboratory (NWREL) serves Alaska, Idaho, Montana, Oregon, and Washington; however, the information here is of value to principals throughout the nation. In addition to research and development, this lab focuses on school re-egineering; quality teaching and learning; student assessment; literacy and language development; and school, family, and community partnerships. The lab also provides field services to state and local education agencies within its service area.

**HIGHLIGHTS FOR PRINCIPALS.** The online Catalog of School Reform Models is an excellent resource offering entire school models, as well as those focusing on reading and language arts. The links in the matrix take you directly to specific information about each model. To access the catalog, go to the **Programs & Projects** area, then select **School Improvement Program**. Or go directly to **www.nwrel.org/scpd/catalog/index.shtml**. The **Topics** section provides a categorized listing of laboratory resources. While visiting **Topics**, be sure to browse the Administration and Management area.

## Pacific Resources for Education and Learning

www.prel.org

**SITE DESCRIPTION.** One of 10 regional laboratories across the country, the Pacific Resources for Education and Learning (PREL) serves several Pacific island political entities; however, the information here is of value to principals throughout the nation. In addition to research and development, this lab's area of emphasis is curriculum and instruction related to reading and language mastery. PREL work also emphasizes multicultural and multilingual education. The lab provides field services to state and local education agencies within its service area.

**HIGHLIGHTS FOR PRINCIPALS.** The most direct way to navigate this site is by clicking the **PREL's Programs** link on the home page and then selecting the programs of interest to you. Most program pages include links to an overview and a description of products and services. You can also access other PREL Web sites, such as **earlyreading.info**, from links on the home page.

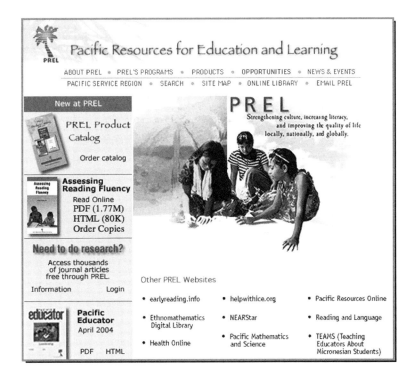

## RAND Education

**www.rand.org/education/**

**SITE DESCRIPTION.** RAND is a nonprofit organization that conducts research and analysis to help policymakers and decision makers do their work. One of the organization's areas of expertise is education. This link takes you directly to the education area of the site, where you can access research reports and publications. All materials are accessible online, or print versions can be ordered for a fee.

**HIGHLIGHTS FOR PRINCIPALS.** RAND's areas of emphasis in education are assessment and accountability, school reform evaluation, and teachers and teaching. When you need information in any of these three areas, click on the **Publications** link, and then on the **Index of all RAND Education Publications** link. This takes you to a page where you may browse the publications by topic or scroll through the alphabetical listing. The online documents are in PDF format. (If you're not familiar with PDF files, refer to the Personal Productivity section of this directory to learn about Adobe Reader, a free program you can download to read PDF files.)

## Southeast Regional Vision for Education

www.serve.org

**SITE DESCRIPTION.** One of 10 regional laboratories across the country, the Southeast Regional Vision for Education (SERVE) serves Alabama, Florida, Georgia, Mississippi, North Carolina, and South Carolina; however, the information here is of value to principals throughout the nation. In addition to research and development, this lab's national leadership focus is expanded learning opportunities, such as prekindergarten and extended-day programs. The lab also provides field services to state and local education agencies within its service area.

**HIGHLIGHTS FOR PRINCIPALS.** If you're looking for information about expanded learning opportunities, visit the **National Leadership Area** of this site, which offers links to Web sites and publications. SERVE also offers complimentary copies of an excellent series of video programs that focus on the use of technology in the classroom. You'll find these in the **Publications** section (click the link at the top of the page) under **Technology, Mathematics, and Science.**

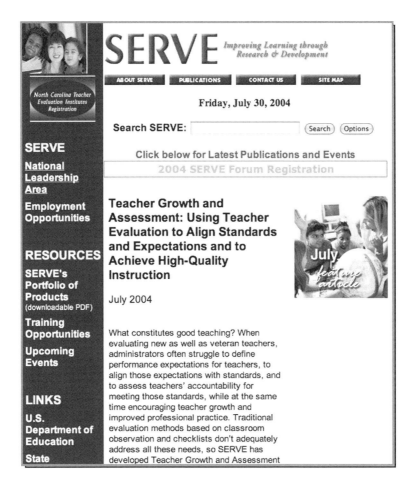

## Southwest Educational Development Laboratory

**www.sedl.org**

**SITE DESCRIPTION.** One of 10 regional laboratories across the country, the Southwest Educational Development Laboratory (SEDL) serves Arkansas, Louisiana, New Mexico, Oklahoma, and Texas; however, the information here is of value to principals throughout the nation. In addition to research and development, this lab's national leadership focus is family and community connections with schools. The lab also provides field services to state and local education agencies within its service area.

**HIGHLIGHTS FOR PRINCIPALS.** Although you can browse **Products** by title or subject, you may find that it's easiest to locate what you're looking for by clicking on **Our Work**, then on **Focus Areas**. Each area is nicely organized, providing an overview, information about current and past work, and links to resources. Be sure to check out the area that discusses involving families and the community in student learning.

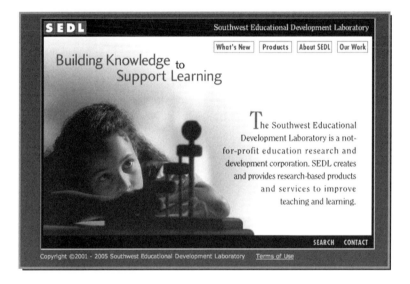

## WestEd

**www.wested.org**

**SITE DESCRIPTION.** One of 10 regional laboratories across the country, the WestEd's primary service area is Arizona, California, Nevada, and Utah; however, the information here is of value to principals throughout the nation. In addition to research and development, this lab's national leadership focus is assessment of educational achievement. The lab also provides field services to state and local education agencies within its service area.

**HIGHLIGHTS FOR PRINCIPALS.** You can access a catalog of publications and other products by clicking on **Products & Resources**, then choosing to browse by author or subject. You can also learn more about each project under WestEd by clicking on **Areas of Work**, then selecting your area of interest, such as **Technology** or **Evaluation**. Each of these subjects has a page that provides an overview, as well as links to related programs and descriptions of services. A wealth of information on assessment can be found at this site.

# Social and Legal Issues

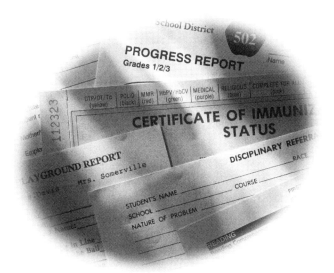

In addition to the curricular and instructional issues they address every day, principals must provide staff and students with a safe and orderly working environment. The four Web sites included in this section of the directory offer information to help you prevent school violence, write and implement comprehensive school safety plans, keep tabs on special education law, and stay up-to-date on federal legislation that pertains to education.

Because each state has its own codes for education, no attempt is made here to address state law. Visit your state's department of education Web site for further information. You can quickly access these sites by going to **www.ed.gov/Programs/bastmp/SEA.htm**. Look for your state's name, and click on the link provided. You might also try a Google search by entering the name of your state and the words "Education Code." For example, type in "Florida Education Code" or "California Education Code."

You might also want to visit the Clearinghouse on Educational Policy and Management at **eric.uoregon.edu**. Under **Trends and Issues**, click on the topic **School Law**. More information about this site is provided in the section of this directory titled General.

# QUICK REFERENCE CHART

| NAME OF SITE/INTERNET ADDRESS | PRIMARY AREA OF EMPHASIS | | | |
| --- | --- | --- | --- | --- |
| | SAFETY PLANNING | CRISIS RESPONSE | SPECIAL EDUCATION LAW | FEDERAL LAW |
| Center for the Prevention of School Violence (CPSV) **www.ncdjjdp.org/cpsv/** | ▓ | ▓ | | |
| Federal Register **www.gpoaccess.gov/fr/** | | | ▓ | ▓ |
| NEA Crisis Communications Guide & Toolkit **www.nea.org/crisis/** | ▓ | ▓ | | |
| Office of Special Education and Rehabilitative Services **www.ed.gov/about/offices/list/osers/osep/** | | | ▓ | ▓ |

## Center for the Prevention of School Violence

**www.ncdjjdp.org/cpsv/**

**SITE DESCRIPTION.** Sponsored by the North Carolina Department of Juvenile Justice and Delinquency Prevention, the Center for the Prevention of School Violence (CPSV) was established in 1993. CPSV serves as a resource center and think tank for promoting safe schools and positive youth development. Resources provided include materials for parents, teachers, school administrators, counselors, and students.

**HIGHLIGHTS FOR PRINCIPALS.** Enter the site by clicking on the building graphic on the home page. There's a lot here, and it will take time to find all the gems. This is a site you may want to visit on an as-needed basis. Start with the **Principal's Office**, where you'll find information on school safety planning and crisis response, as well as suggestions for additional steps principals can take to increase school safety. From there you may want to go to the **Facilities** area to learn about how the physical appearance of your school impacts the community's perception of safety, or perhaps to the **Journalism Department**, where you'll find newsletters and other publications about school safety. Bookmark the site and return to it whenever a safety issue arises.

## Federal Register

**www.gpoaccess.gov/fr/**

**SITE DESCRIPTION.** The *Federal Register* is a daily publication of notices from federal agencies and organizations. It also includes presidential executive orders and other documents. The searchable database goes back to 1994.

**HIGHLIGHTS FOR PRINCIPALS.** Knowing about this site comes in handy when you need to track down information on a federal act such as No Child Left Behind. Be sure to read the search directions carefully; taking the time to review them makes database searching much easier.

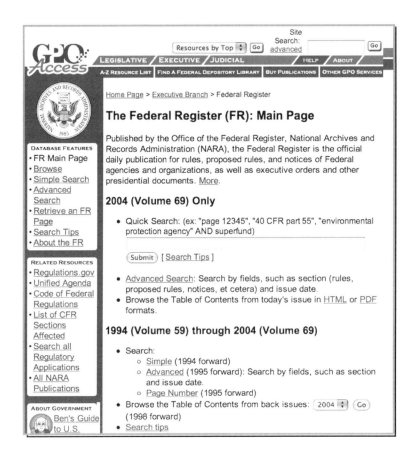

## NEA Crisis Communications Guide & Toolkit

**www.nea.org/crisis/**

**SITE DESCRIPTION.** Developed by the National Education Association (NEA), this comprehensive guide and toolkit covers what needs to be done before a crisis, what to do during a crisis, and how to deal with the aftermath of a crisis. It provides 33 tools you can use to plan for, and meet, a crisis.

**HIGHLIGHTS FOR PRINCIPALS.** Download, print, and use material from this resource as a ready reference. It's valuable for revising your own school safety plan and for establishing procedures for emergency drills.

## Office of Special Education and Rehabilitative Services
www.ed.gov/about/offices/list/osers/osep/

**SITE DESCRIPTION.** The Office of Special Education and Rehabilitative Services provides leadership and financial support to assist educators in meeting the needs of students with disabilities. The site is a resource for information about the Individuals with Disabilities Education Act (IDEA) and about federal programs and initiatives that support individuals with disabilities.

**HIGHLIGHTS FOR PRINCIPALS.** The **History** of IDEA link offers a quick overview of the impact of IDEA during the last 25 years. The IDEA—The **Law and Regulations** link leads to a page where you can access the actual legislation. Find contact information for parent training and information opportunities in your state by clicking on the **Parent-Training and Information Centers** link. This area also features links to helpful resources that address **No Child Left Behind**, **Scientifically Based Research**, and the **What Works Clearinghouse**.

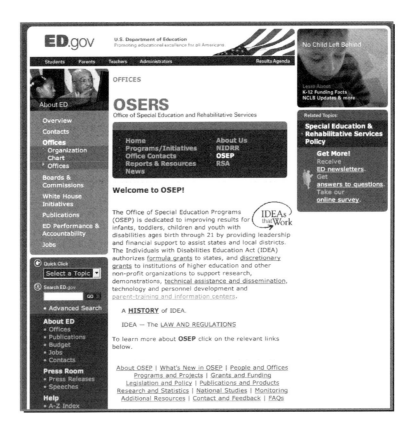

# Technology Use

**M**any educators struggle with technology use that goes beyond simple automation of basic tasks. Your leadership is vital to helping teachers implement technology as an instructional tool. The Web sites in this section provide background information to help you:

- develop or refine your own vision for technology use at your school

- implement technology-based instruction, taking costs into account

- review research related to technology use in schools

The Regional Technology in Education Consortia (R*TEC) sites, coupled with the Technology Information Center for Administrative Leadership (TICAL) site, are places you should revisit regularly to review updates and changes in the instructional technology landscape.

Additional instructional technology-related sites are listed in this directory in the sections titled Professional Organizations, Professional Reading, and Research Institutes and Education Centers.

# QUICK REFERENCE CHART

| NAME OF SITE/INTERNET ADDRESS | PRIMARY AREA OF EMPHASIS | | | | | |
| --- | --- | --- | --- | --- | --- | --- |
| | TECHNOLOGY USE IN THE U.S. | BUDGETING FOR TECH-NOLOGY | INTERNET SAFETY | NEW TECHNOLO-GIES | PLANNING FOR TECH-NOLOGY USE | REFERENCE AND WEB SITES |
| Center for Applied Research in Educational Technology (CARET) **caret.iste.org** | ■ | | | | ■ | ■ |
| Consortium for School Networking (CoSN) **www.cosn.org** | | ■ | ■ | | | |
| Educator's Reference Desk: Educational Technology **www.eduref.org/cgi-bin/res.cgi/ Educational_Technology** | | | | | ■ | ■ |
| Network of Regional Technology in Education Consortia (R*TEC) **www.rtec.org** | | ■ | ■ | ■ | ■ | ■ |
| Partnership for 21st Century Skills **www.21stcenturyskills.org** | | | | | ■ | ■ |
| Pew Internet & American Life Project **www.pewinternet.org** | ■ | | | | | |
| Technology Information Center for Administrative Leadership (TICAL) **www.portical.org** | | ■ | ■ | ■ | ■ | ■ |

## Center for Applied Research in Educational Technology

caret.iste.org

**SITE DESCRIPTION.** The International Society for Technology in Education (ISTE) is working in partnership with Educational Support Systems (ESS) in San Mateo, California, to develop a searchable database of research studies and other information about technology use in education. The Sacramento County Office of Education created the site, called the Center for Applied Research in Educational Technology (CARET). The effort is funded by the Bill and Melinda Gates Foundation.

**HIGHLIGHTS FOR PRINCIPALS.** You can access the information in several ways. By clicking on **Browse Questions & Answers**, you'll find links to research focused on student learning, curriculum and instruction, online teaching and learning, professional development, and assessment and evaluation. Click on the topic area of interest, and you'll find a list of hyperlinked questions. By clicking on a question, you're taken directly to information answering the question. For example, learn more about how teacher technology standards can be met by clicking on **Professional Development** and then clicking on the question about teacher technology standards. You can also access information by using the search option, which returns results based on keywords you enter or study characteristics you select.

## Consortium for School Networking

www.cosn.org

**SITE DESCRIPTION.** The Consortium for School Networking (CoSN) promotes the use of the Internet and telecommunications to improve K–12 student learning. While much of the material is directed toward district, state, and national levels, four areas of interest to school principals are listed in the left-hand column:

- **Taking TCO to the Classroom:** Budgeting for technology

- **Safeguarding the Wired Schoolhouse:** Understanding the issues in managing Internet content

- **Data-Driven Decision Making:** Using data to increase student achievement

- **Student Tech Support:** Engaging students in on-site technical support

**HIGHLIGHTS FOR PRINCIPALS.** Visit the areas mentioned above. **Taking TCO to the Classroom** offers an overview of the concept of Total Cost of Ownership (TCO) and how it affects schools. The **Publications & Tools** section within this area features downloadable materials, including a report, a chart for determining your TCO needs, and a PowerPoint presentation you can use with staff or planning groups. The same kinds of materials are available in **Safeguarding the Wired Schoolhouse**, with a focus on managing Internet content. **Data-Driven Decision Making** offers publications and tools to help educators better understand how to use data as a tool to increase student achievement. **Student Tech Support** provides a guide for site leaders who are considering implementation of a formal program where students assist with on-site technical support.

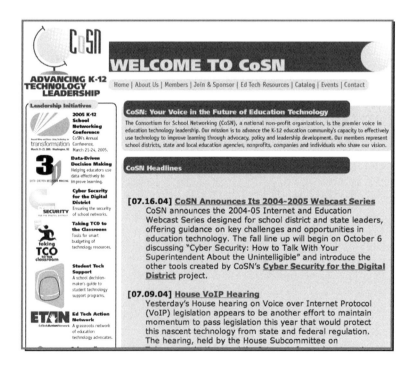

## Educator's Reference Desk: Educational Technology

www.eduref.org/cgi-bin/res.cgi/Educational_Technology

**SITE DESCRIPTION.** With the demise of the 16 Educational Resources Information Center (ERIC) clearinghouses, many of the resources have been moved to the Educator's Reference Desk. This link takes you to the Educational Technology section. The collection is organized into several categories, including **Computers**, **Distance Education**, **Instructional Issues**, and **Technology Planning**. Each category offers links to Internet sites, and several also offer links to online communities and organizations.

**HIGHLIGHTS FOR PRINCIPALS.** The extensive resource links provided are very helpful. Several areas offer Archived Responses to Ask ERIC questions. The responses include links to ERIC article summaries and other online resources. This site is a good starting point for exploring additional Web sites and publications.

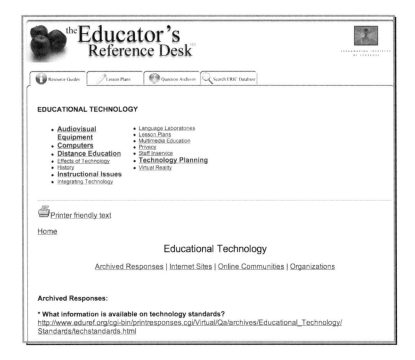

## Network of Regional Technology in Education Consortia

**www.rtec.org**

**SITE DESCRIPTION.** The Network of Regional Technology in Education Consortia (R*TEC) is funded by the U.S. Department of Education. The 10 national R*TEC Centers serve regions aligned with the 10 national Regional Education Laboratories. The purpose of these centers is to help educators effectively use advanced technologies in the classroom. You can access any of the individual centers from this page and also find highlights of products and resources available from all the centers.

**HIGHLIGHTS FOR PRINCIPALS.** Visit the **R*TEC Resources and Products** area (from the link at the bottom of the page) to get a quick overview of materials available through the various centers. You'll find publications, surveys, technology planning and training materials, and more. The **Education Technology NEWS** area (in the left-hand menu) is great for getting a quick update on hot topics in educational technology.

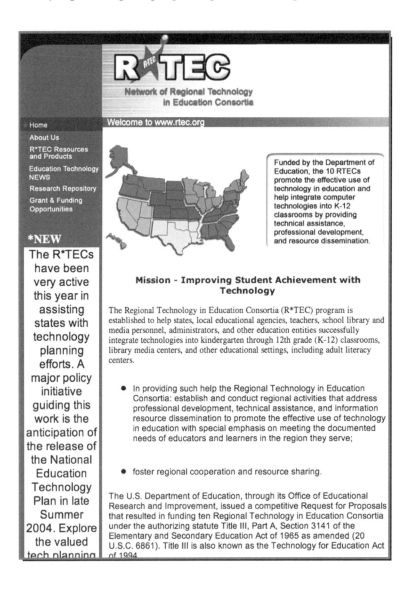

## Partnership for 21st Century Skills

www.21stcenturyskills.org

**SITE DESCRIPTION.** This organization, whose members include public and private groups, focuses on helping communities better prepare students for the 21st century in terms of the workplace and society. The site offers reports and publications along with resources and tools for educators.

**HIGHLIGHTS FOR PRINCIPALS.** The Home page features links to new materials. Current spotlights include **Route 21: An Interactive Guide to 21st Century Learning**, **The Road to 21st Century Learning: A Policymaker's Guide to 21st Century Skills**, and a series of maps called **ICT Literacy Maps**. Along with the featured links, be sure to visit **Reports & Publications**, where you'll find materials helpful in developing your vision for 21st-century learning. **Resources & Tools** provides information useful as you work with staff to integrate 21st-century skills into the classroom.

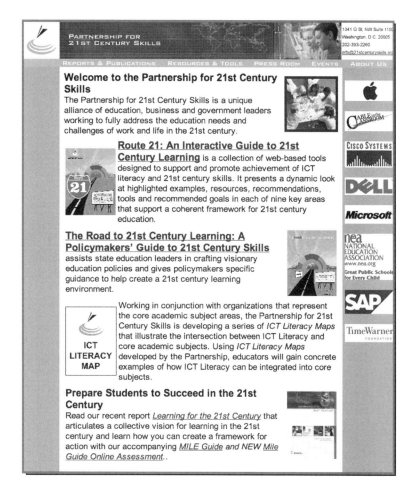

## Pew Internet & American Life Project

**www.pewinternet.org**

**SITE DESCRIPTION.** This project explores the impact of Internet use on American life. Reports examine changes in family life, home and work, education, communities, and more. The project also monitors the evolution of the Internet itself.

**HIGHLIGHTS FOR PRINCIPALS.** Internet use continues to be one of the most rapidly growing forms of technology use. While it's possible that schools can help bridge the "digital divide" when students have limited home access, it's also true that many educational institutions are themselves lagging behind. This Web site is an excellent resource for current information about the Internet and its impact on American society. In addition to accessing reports, you'll find online presentations, data, and Pew's latest findings on trends.

## Technology Information Center for Administrative Leadership
www.portical.org

**SITE DESCRIPTION.** A special project funded by the California Department of Education, the Technology Information Center for Administrative Leadership (TICAL) Web site targets school administrators and their technology needs. Hundreds of resources reviewed by experienced educators are available. These include:

- **Tools & Templates:** From the link at the top of the page, go to ready-to-use productivity tools you can download or access online.

- **Features:** From the listing on the left, visit the **Expert Opinion** link for articles and presentations on topics such as data-driven decision making, curriculum integration, financial planning, and operations.

- **Interact:** Also accessible from the left-hand menu, **Interact** offers online surveys and forums as well as opportunities to provide feedback and ask questions.

- **Resource Database:** The heart of this site has search capabilities or point-and-click tables for searching specific resources for technology implementation at your school.

**HIGHLIGHTS FOR PRINCIPALS.** In **Tools & Templates**, you will find many useful items. Visit **Technology Planning** in **Tools & Templates** to find planning templates suitable for use in staff and committee meetings. Try the **Matrix Search** in the **Resource Database** to take the guesswork out of finding online resources geared to your technology needs. Just specify the topic you're interested in and the type of resource you're looking for. One matrix page is aligned to the National Educational Technology Standards for Administrators (NETS•A).

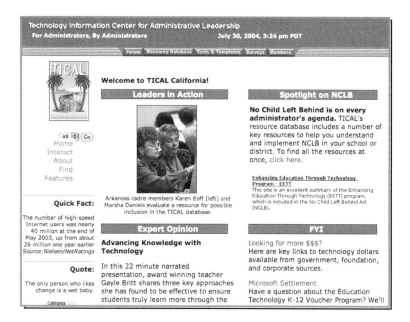

CHAPTER 1
Hardware and
Connections

CHAPTER 2
Internet and
World Wide Web
Basics

# PART 2

## INTERNET
## SURVIVAL
## SKILLS

CHAPTER 3
Beyond the Basics

CHAPTER 4
Internet Security

# INTRODUCTION TO PART 2

**Please note:** Chapters 1 and 2 of part 2 are designed to help beginning Internet users get online successfully. Seasoned Internet users who are helping fellow principals learn about the Internet may want to use the material here as a guide. If you're interested in learning more advanced Internet skills, refer to part 2, chapter 3.

My goal is to encourage principals to use the Internet, a powerful source of information and ideas that can make the site administrator's job more manageable. However, my experience working with school administrators tells me that principals often do not take advantage of Internet resources. This happens for a variety of reasons, but usually it boils down to three factors:

- hardware issues, including inadequate computer equipment or a slow Internet connection

- software problems due to a lack of familiarity with Web browsers, search engines, and the like

- lack of familiarity with information and resources available online

When your computer equipment isn't up to snuff or you don't understand how to use the software provided to get around the Internet and World Wide Web, you can waste a lot of time—not an attractive proposition for most principals. Just one or two unhappy experiences are enough to deter many principals from using the Internet in their professional lives. Much of this difficulty can be avoided, or at least significantly reduced, with basic information about equipment and software.

The information provided in chapter 1, "Hardware and Connections," and chapter 2, "Internet and World Wide Web Basics," will help you access the Web sites listed in part 1, "Directory of Internet Sites." Chapter 3 contains information for more advanced users. Following is a brief summary of the three chapters.

- **Chapter 1—Hardware and Connections** deals with the physical setup you need to actually get online. If you already have this capability at home and are happy with your connection speed, move on to chapter 2. If you'll be accessing the Internet through a high-speed connection at school, again skip to chapter 2. However, if you're just getting set up to go online at school or home, are using a telephone line for your connection, or don't have a clue what this paragraph means, you need to start with chapter 1. The material here won't make you a tech guru, but it will provide the information you need to get started.

- **Chapter 2—Internet and World Wide Web Basics** explains how to get online and the basics for accessing Web sites once you're connected to the Internet. There's also a section that identifies common problems new Internet users face, with simple remedies so that your time spent online is productive and satisfying.

- **Chapter 3—Beyond the Basics** is for readers who want to use more than one Internet browser, work with multiple browser windows, and organize and maintain lists of favorite Web sites and page. Information about how to conduct productive Internet searches to find additional Web sites is also provided.

- **Chapter 4—Internet Security** covers the most common security threats that Internet users are prey to, and discusses what you can do to protect yourself. T he sources and habits of a menagerie of malware—viruses, worms, Trojan horsees, and browser hijackers—are described, and basic countermeasures that promote safe surfing are provided.

## CHAPTER 1

# Hardware and Connections

Will you be using the Internet at school? At home? Both? Your equipment, connection, and Internet service provider (ISP) needs will be different at each location.

Thanks to E-rate, most schools now offer computer networks where Internet access is available through a high-speed connection. If this is true at your school, you don't need to worry about basic hardware and connection issues at work and may want to skip this chapter. However, if your school doesn't have a network and a high-speed connection, or if you want to access the Internet from home, read on.

To keep things simple, the information presented here assumes you're considering an Internet connection from home. However, if you need a telephone connection to the Internet at school, the advice in this chapter also applies. To get online using a stand-alone computer, your *minimum* needs are:

- a computer
- a modem
- a telephone line
- an ISP

## COMPUTER

Today's Web sites make heavy use of graphics, sound, animation, and text. Newer computers are better equipped to handle these sites because they have faster processors, more memory, and better graphics management. You don't need a crash course on computer specifications, but you do want to use a computer that's capable of handling the Web pages you want to access. If your computer is less than three years old, you should be fine. If your computer is older, you may have difficulty.

Seek advice from your school's or district's computer technician. Provide the technician with the make and model of your computer system or bring your owner's manual when you meet. Explain that you're interested in using the Internet in your work and ask whether your current computer system is up to the job. If it is, the technician can quickly determine this. If not, he or she may be able to recommend inexpensive upgrades that would allow you to successfully access the Internet. If your computer is too old to upgrade, you may need to purchase a newer model before you can use the Internet easily from home.

In that case, if you have an adequate setup at school, I'd recommend that you first spend some time learning how to access Web sites there. Getting some Internet experience under your belt using school equipment can help you decide whether you actually want to make an investment in a new computer or other equipment for use at home.

## MODEM

The modem is a device that enables your computer to communicate with the Internet. If your home computer doesn't already have a modem, the computer is probably too old and slow for today's Internet demands. New computers typically come with at least a V.90 56K modem installed. The numbers refer to the speed of data transfer. This modem enables you to use a regular telephone line to connect with the Internet.

Although it's possible to do so, you don't want to use a modem with a top speed that's less than 56K, because data transmission will slow to a crawl. If your current modem's top speed capability is less than 56K, talk with your technician about options for replacing it.

If you decide to use a different type of connection, such as cable, DSL (digital subscriber line), or satellite, the company you contract with will provide a special modem for you to use, even if you have a V.90 56K modem. This special modem will require installation. It's worth your while to pay the installation fee and have the company install it for you.

---

**VOCABULARY TERMS**

**modem**

Stands for **mod**ulator-**dem**odulator. This device may be external (outside your computer) or internal (usually a card plugged into a slot inside your computer). The modem converts data stored on your computer into a format that can be transferred via telephone or cable lines. Different modems send and receive data at different speeds. Generally, the faster the better.

**cable modem**

A modem designed to send and receive data through television cable networks. Data transmission speed is very fast, but the technology is still being refined. Cable Internet service is not available in all areas or through all cable companies.

**DSL**

Short for digital subscriber line. DSL offers subscribers a high-speed Internet connection through telephone lines. DSL is not available in all areas, and access depends on the subscriber's proximity to telephone switching stations.

---

# INTERNET ACCESS

You can use your existing telephone line to access the Internet. This is called a dial-up connection. The advantage is that it doesn't cost more to do this unless you have to make a toll or long distance call to your ISP. However, there are disadvantages. In many instances, using your existing telephone line means you can't make or receive phone calls when you or someone else in your home is logged on to the Internet. You must either install a second phone line or pay for special services (available in only some areas) that offer more flexible use of one phone line. Also, data transmission over regular telephone lines is slow. Because of this, it's not uncommon for users to be disconnected while attempting to access Web pages. Educators I work with who use dial-up connections frequently express frustration about slow-loading Web sites, being knocked offline, and other problems.

In many areas, it's now possible to connect to the Internet from home using DSL, cable, or a satellite connection. DSL and cable options are fairly inexpensive (as little as $40 per month), and both provide much faster service than a dial-up connection. Broadband satellite Internet connections are more expensive but are an option for users in areas where DSL or cable isn't available. Even though a DSL connection uses your telephone line, you can still make and receive telephone calls while online. Another advantage of DSL, cable, and satellite is that you don't need to pay an additional fee for a commercial ISP because these services connect you directly to the Internet. DSL and cable also offer e-mail services to customers. When you factor in the cost of maintaining a second phone line, DSL and cable aren't much more expensive than a dial-up connection.

# INTERNET SERVICE PROVIDER

If you're using a telephone line dial-up connection to access the Internet, you must have an account with an ISP. As mentioned, this service is included when you have a DSL, cable, or satellite connection because your computer connects directly to the Internet each time you turn it on. When you sign up for an ISP account, you receive software, a user name, a password, and an access telephone number. Once the software is installed on your computer, it's usually simple to follow the directions provided to log on to the Internet. Your ISP should offer technical assistance via telephone in case you encounter any problems getting online. Write down the telephone number for their help line and keep it next to your computer.

Well-known commercial ISPs include America Online and Earthlink. Many more are available. It's often possible to pick up a free copy of ISP software at a retail electronics store, install the software, and open your account online.

Unless you live in an isolated area, you should be able to find an ISP that offers its customers a local access number. This is important. If you must use a number that's a long-distance call, your telephone bill will reflect these charges, which mount up very quickly. Therefore, it's important that new Internet users determine right away if their access number is a long-distance call to avoid accruing enormous telephone bills.

**VOCABULARY TERM**

**ISP**

Short for Internet service provider. These companies provide access to the Internet for a monthly fee. A dial-up connection to the Internet requires that a user go through an ISP to access the Internet.

CHAPTER 2

# Internet and World Wide Web Basics

G etting online is easy. Once there, how do you find the information you need? The information in the following chapter applies whether you're on a PC, on a Mac, at work, or at home.

Although people often use the terms Internet and World Wide Web interchangeably, as you can see from the definitions provided here, they really aren't synonymous.

---

**VOCABULARY TERMS**

**Internet**

The Internet provides the network infrastructure that enables millions of computers around the world to connect to one another for communication purposes.

**World Wide Web**

The World Wide Web is one source of information for Internet users, but it is not the Internet itself. It uses the Internet network to allow people to access Web sites.

---

Once you have established a connection to the Internet, you use a Web browser to actually view Web sites.

---

**VOCABULARY TERM**

**Web browser**

A software program (application) used to access Web pages. Some ISPs (such as America Online) provide their own Web browser. Other ISPs use commonly available Web browsers, usually Internet Explorer or Netscape. Most newer computer systems come with Internet Explorer or Netscape already installed.

---

# LOGGING ON

When using a dial-up connection, you first connect to the Internet through your ISP. Some ISPs, such as AOL, have their own browsers to navigate the Web. Your ISP should provide you with instructions on how to set up your modem and any necessary software. When you connect through a DSL, cable, or other high-speed connection (common for most schools), you're usually taken immediately to the Internet when you launch your Web browser program. Simply turn on the computer and you'll be connected to the Internet.

Either way, to actually view sites, you need to open your Web browser software. Common browsers include Internet Explorer (which comes with Windows), Safari (which comes with Mac OS X), Netscape, or Mozilla Firefox.

1. Find the icon for your Web browser on the computer desktop (Figure 1). Open the software by double-clicking on the icon.

FIGURE 1. These desktop icons are for two different Web browsers, Netscape and Internet Explorer. To open either program, double-click on the icon.

*If you do not see an icon on your desktop:*

**For PCs:** Click on Start in the Windows Taskbar. Scroll to highlight Programs or All Programs. A pop-up menu listing all programs installed on your computer will appear. Highlight the name of your Web browser and click (Figure 2).

**For Macs:** Double-click on the hard drive icon on your desktop. You'll see folders for information stored on your hard drive, including one called Applications, also listed on the left. Your Web browser will be listed, along with its icon. Open the Applications folder. Double-click on the name to open the program (Figure 3).

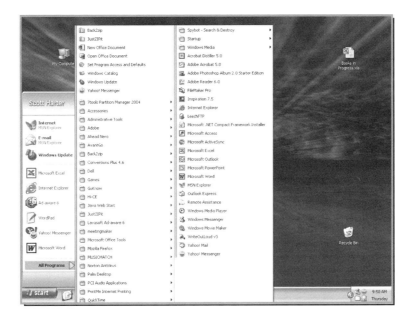

FIGURE 2. Using Start and Programs to find your Web browser on a PC.

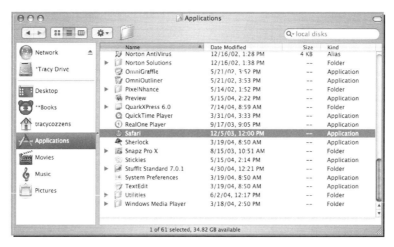

FIGURE 3. Finding the Web browser through the Applications folder on a Mac.

**3.** Once the Web browser is open, the software connects to the Internet.

**4.** When the Internet connection is made, you'll see your current home page (Figure 4). This page can be changed through the browser software. When using Internet Explorer on the PC, go to the Tools menu, select Internet Options, then the General tab. On the Mac, access the Preferences box through the menu under the software's name.

---

**VOCABULARY TERM**

**home page**

The main page of a Web site, which usually has several links to other sections of the site.

---

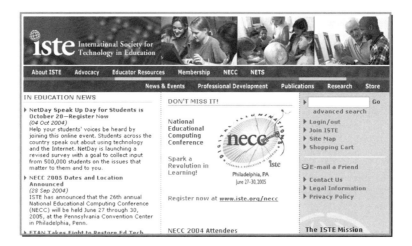

FIGURE 4. Example of a home page (in this case, the International Society for Technology in Education). You can set your home page to any page on the Internet.

# USING A WEB BROWSER

## Overview of the Web Browser Window

Although a number of Web browsers are available, the windows are remarkably similar in design. For the sake of simplicity, the following figures and discussion use Internet Explorer as an example. However, the information presented is applicable to Web browsers in general. Figure 5 identifies the common toolbars found on a Web browser window.

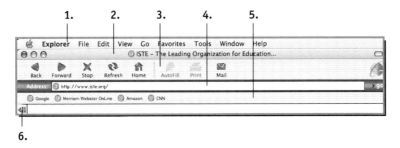

FIGURE 5. Internet Explorer toolbars.

1. **Menu bar.** These drop-down menus have commands for using all of the program's features.

2. **Title bar.** The name of the Web page that is open appears here.

3. **Standard toolbar.** The buttons on this toolbar provide the basic tools you need to use the Web browser.

4. **Address bar.** This is where you type addresses for Web sites.

5. **Links bar.** These are direct links to sites of interest. The default sites are Microsoft-related, but you can customize the bar with your own special links.

6. **Expand or collapse button.** Click here to collapse the toolbars and enlarge the viewing space. To restore the toolbars, click the button again.

In addition to the toolbars, you'll want to use other features of the Web browser window. Figure 6 points out these features.

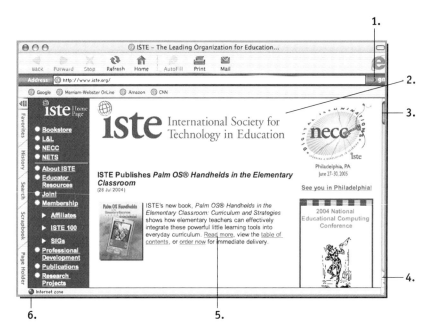

FIGURE 6. Web browser window features.

1. **Go button.** When a Web site address is typed in the address window, clicking the Go button takes you to the site.

2. **Browser window.** This is the area where Web pages are displayed.

3. **Scroll bar.** Click and drag the box in the bar to move the page displayed in the browser window up or down.

4. **Scroll-up and scroll-down arrows.** Click on these arrows to scroll the page displayed in the browser window up or down.

5. **Link.** Links are very powerful. They enable you to move from one Web page to another or one section of a site to another. Links appear as text or graphics. To find a link, move your cursor across the browser window. Whenever the cursor changes to a hand icon, it's pointing at a link. Text links are usually easy to identify because the text will be underlined and a different color. To access a link and view additional pages, click when the hand icon appears.

6. **Connectivity icon.** When you see this icon, it indicates you are online.

# UNDERSTANDING WEB SITE ADDRESSES

## The Anatomy of a Web Site Address

Before learning more about browser tools, it's important to understand the structure of Web site addresses, or URLs. This is because you use the browser tools in conjunction with the Web site addresses you enter into the address bar. Web site addresses are often confusing to work with if you don't understand the naming conventions.

---

**VOCABULARY TERMS**

**URL**

An abbreviation for uniform resource locator. Every file on the Internet has a unique address, or URL, assigned to it so that you can find the file. URLs have two parts. The first part identifies the protocol, or format, of the file. Web page URLs usually begin with "http." The second part of the URL is the domain name, which identifies where the Web page you want is stored.

**domain name**

A domain name is part of an Internet address, or URL.

---

Let's take a closer look at an actual URL (Figure 7).

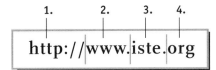

FIGURE 7. Sample URL.

1. **Protocol.** This identifies the format of the file you're accessing. Most Web pages begin with http://, which means hypertext transfer protocol. You may encounter two other protocols:

   - **https://** indicates a secure Web site where steps have been taken to protect data.

   - **ftp://** means file transfer protocol and indicates that a file has been uploaded on an ftp server. This file can be downloaded in full by a computer that accesses the ftp address.

Parts 2–4 comprise the **domain name**. Here's what each part means:

2. **www.** This part of the domain name stands for World Wide Web, the host server for this site. Most, but not all, URLs include this.

3. **Second-level domain.** The second-level domain is the portion of a URL that identifies the specific and unique administrative owner associated with the site. In the example above, **iste** tells you that the International Society for Technology in Education owns the Web site.

4. **Top-level domain.** The top-level domain identifies the most general part of the domain name in an Internet address. It's important because it provides information about the origin of a Web page. You can use this information to help determine the credibility of a Web page. The number of suffixes is limited. The most common are:

.**gov**  government

.**edu**  education

.**org**  organization

.**com** commercial

.**net**  network

.**mil**  military

Others are country codes, such as **.fr** for France or **.is** for Iceland. The domain suffix of **.org** in the sample URL tells you that ISTE is an organization.

## Determining a Site's Credibility

How can you use this information to determine site credibility? Look at the two imaginary Internet addresses below:

- http://www.excellentuniversity.edu
- http://www.excellentuniversity.com

Which address is more likely to provide objective information? Probably the address ending in **edu**, because this tells you it's an educational institution. The address ending in **com** tells you this is a commercial site.

Many of the URLs you find in this directory will have additional information beyond the domain name. This is because the domain name alone takes you to the Web site home page. Additional information will take you further into the site, bypassing the home page. For example, the URL **http://teacher.scholastic.com/professional/grants/school_fund_raising.htm** takes you beyond Scholastic's home page for teachers (**teacher.scholastic.com**) and directly to an article titled "School Fund-Raising Activities That Work."

## Entering a URL

To enter a new URL, you must first clear the URL already in the address bar. Do this by pointing at the URL and clicking once. This will highlight the existing URL (Figure 8).

FIGURE 8. Highlighting an existing URL.

When the existing URL is highlighted, you can begin typing the new Web address. Be very careful as you type the address. Include all punctuation marks and check the spelling. The URL must be entered correctly to successfully access the Web site.

If you make a mistake, you can click once to highlight the text in the address bar and start over. You can also correct an error by pointing at the mistake and clicking twice. This causes a flashing cursor to appear in the address bar where you've pointed. You can then edit the URL by using the backspace (or delete) key and retyping. To edit a URL, use the same techniques you use while editing in a word processing program.

Once the URL is correctly typed, press Enter or click on the Go button to access the new Web site (Figure 9).

FIGURE 9. Go button.

You need to wait for the Web page to download before you can read it. This is when the speed of your connection becomes important. A dial-up connection takes much longer to download a site, especially if the site contains a lot of graphics.

Occasionally, you'll have difficulty opening a Web page. You may see a message that says the page cannot be displayed. Check to make sure you typed the URL correctly. If you made a mistake, retype or edit the URL and try again. If the URL appears to be correct, it's possible the site is temporarily down, the URL has been changed, or the page is no longer available. Wait a while and try the URL again. If you continue to get the error message, read and follow the directions that appear with the message. They'll take you to the site's home page, where you may be able to find the specific information you need.

# ESSENTIAL WEB BROWSER TOOLS

Now that you've opened a Web page, you need to know about the tools you can use to navigate the site and save or print information. Look closely at Figure 10. You see 11 tool buttons here. Some are grayed out, indicating they can't be used until a page or form is loaded. Different buttons appear depending on your browser.

FIGURE 10. Essential Web browser tools.

You can easily customize your toolbar following directions provided by your browser. Start by opening the Help menu. In Internet Explorer, scroll down to Customizing Internet Explorer, then to Customizing Toolbars. In Netscape, scroll down to Customizing Netscape, then Toolbars. In most cases, the various icons can be dragged into your toolbar.

Although you may want to learn more about all the buttons on the toolbar in Figure 10, you really only need to use four to get started: Back, Forward, Favorites, and Print.

## Back and Forward

A common experience for new Internet users is to follow several links in a Web site and suddenly become lost, not knowing how to retrace their steps to return to a previous page. You can move back and forth between pages you've visited using the Back and Forward buttons.

The simplest way to go back and forth is to move page by page. You can do this by clicking on the Back or Forward buttons. Each click moves one page forward or backward, depending on which button you choose (Figure 11).

FIGURE 11. Back and Forward buttons.

The appearance of the buttons tells you whether you have pages to move to. For example, in Figure 11, the Back button is dark and the label is in black text, indicating the button is active and you have Web pages to move back to. The shadowy appearance of the Forward arrow and label indicates the button is inactive because there are no pages to move forward to. This means the Web page displayed is the last page you've visited during this session.

Another technique is to look for small black arrowheads just to the right of the Back and Forward buttons. Depending on your browser, you may not see them. If you don't see them, move your cursor over the icon, and they'll appear. By clicking on the arrowhead to the right of the Back button, you can see a list of the sites you've visited during your current online session. Figure 12 illustrates this.

FIGURE 12. Sample Back list accessed through a drop-down menu.

Highlight a site name in the drop-down list and click. You'll be taken directly to that page.

If you've moved back to a previous page and then decide to revisit a page you just left, use the arrowhead to the right of the Forward button. Figure 13 illustrates this.

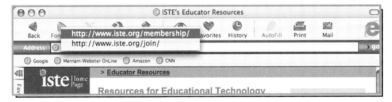

FIGURE 13. Sample Forward list accessed through a drop-down menu.

In this example, the user can choose to move forward to two other pages by highlighting either site name and clicking.

## Favorites

You might find Web sites you want to revisit at a later time. You can't access them from the Back and Forward drop-down menus unless you happened to visit them during the current online session. You could keep a handwritten list of sites next to your computer, but then you'd need to worry about copying URLs accurately and not losing the list!

Fortunately, Web browsers provide an option that allows you to make a list of sites you want to revisit later. Internet Explorer calls these Favorites; Netscape calls these Bookmarks. Clicking on Favorites or Bookmarks in the menu will open a drop-down menu listing your favorite Web sites and pages. From here, you can go directly to a listed site. You can also click on the Bookmarks or Favorites toolbar button to open a window showing a list of your stored sites (Figure 14). In Internet Explorer, another method to access the Favorites window is to click on the Favorites tab at the far left of the browser. No matter how you access the list, you can scroll through it, highlight the name of a site, and click to go directly to that site.

In Internet Explorer, a button allows you to add a site to your list of favorites. Another way to add a site is by accessing the menu. To do this in Internet Explorer, click on Favorites, then select Add Page to Favorites from the drop-down menu. To do this in Netscape, select Bookmarks, then select Bookmark This Page. (Keyboard shortcuts are indicated for these choices, usually Control+D or Command+D.)

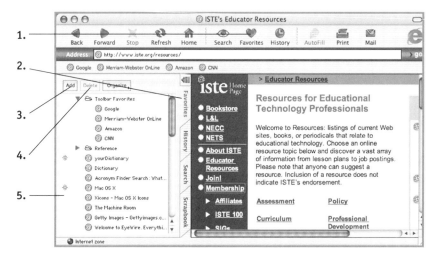

FIGURE 14. Favorites tools in Internet Explorer.

1. **Favorites button.** This button acts like a toggle switch. Click it once and the list of Favorites will appear on the left side of your screen. Click it again, and the list will be hidden.

2. **Favorites tab.** This is another way to open and close the Favorites list.

3. **Add button.** When you're visiting a site you'd like to add to your list of favorites, click on this button and follow the simple directions that appear.

4. **Delete button.** Use the Delete button to delete unwanted sites.

5. **Favorites list.** This is the list of sites you have saved and can visit time after time. Most browsers come installed with certain sites already included in the list.

## Print

At times you'll want to print a site page instead of adding it to your list of favorites. Perhaps you want specific information but doubt you would want to visit the site again at a later time. Printing the Web page currently in the browser window is easy. Simply click on the Print button in the toolbar.

# ANSWERS TO FREQENTLY ASKED QUESTIONS

## CONNECTION ISSUES

**Problem**

You're using a new computer and a fast modem, but the dial-up connection is sometimes sluggish.

**Remedy**

Even with top-of-the-line equipment, if you use a dial-up connection you may be logged on to the Internet at a speed far slower than your equipment can handle. When connecting to the Internet using a dial-up connection and an ISP account, watch as the connection is made to see what the connection speed is. If it's less than 49,333 bps, disconnect and try again.

**Problem**

Your computer is frequently disconnected from the ISP while browsing Web pages or trying to work online.

**Remedy**

You are most likely using an older computer and modem or a dial-up connection. If your equipment is more than three years old, talk with a technician about upgrading or replacing it. Although data transmission is slower over a dial-up computer, newer computers and modems can generally handle graphics-intensive Web sites without being disconnected.

## NAVIGATION ISSUES

**Problem**

"The page cannot be displayed" error message appears on your screen when trying to access a Web page.

**Remedy**

Here are four things to try:

1. Check the spelling and punctuation in the URL. Common mistakes include extra letters (such as wwww instead of www) or missing periods or slash marks. Edit the URL and again click Go.

2. If the URL is correct, the Web site may be down temporarily. Try to access the site later.

3. If the URL is correct, the Web site may have been revised. The error message provides the option of clicking on the site's home page URL. Click on this and look at the home page to try to locate a link that will take you to the information you want.

4. If you click on the home page URL provided on the error page and cannot enter the site, the site may be temporarily down or it may no longer exist.

## NAVIGATION ISSUES (cont.)

**Problem**

You've used links to visit several pages and want to go back to a previous page, but the Back button is not active.

**Remedy**

Some Web pages actually open a new browser window when accessed. If you cannot use the Back button to retrace your steps, click on the black X in the upper right corner of the open window (upper left corner on a Mac). This will close the extra browser window and, in effect, take you back one page, where the Back button should be active.

**Problem**

You've used links to visit several pages and want to go back to a previous page. The Back button is active, but when you click on it, you don't move back to the previous page.

**Remedy**

This is called "mousetrapping." Some sites intentionally try to make it difficult for you to use the Back button to leave the site. Usually you can go back by being persistent and clicking the mouse several times. If this doesn't work, you may need to type in a URL and press Enter, or click Go to leave.

## FAVORITES ISSUES

**Problem**

You've added a home page to your list of favorite Web sites but can't find the specific link you wanted within the site.

**Remedy**

When you want to return to a particular place in a Web site at a later time, you can add that specific page to your list of favorites by clicking the Add button when you're viewing that page. Home pages of Web sites that are frequently updated may not continue to feature a specific link, and it can be very difficult to retrace your steps later.

**Problem**

You've developed a lengthy list of favorite Web sites, but the titles they're saved under mean nothing to you so you don't remember which is which.

**Remedy**

When you add a site to your list of favorites, it will appear as the last title in the list. You can highlight the name, right click one time, and select Rename from the drop-down menu that appears. You can then give the site a name that will be more meaningful to you later.

**Problem**

Today at school you added a site to your list of favorites, but it doesn't appear on the list on your computer at home.

**Remedy**

A list of favorite sites stored on one computer can't be accessed on any other computer because this information is stored in a file on your hard drive. If you find a site at school that you want to work with at home (or anywhere else), the easiest way to handle it is to copy and paste the URL into an e-mail and send it to your home e-mail address. If the hotlink is active when you open the e-mail, click on it and you'll go straight to that page. If not, copy the URL and paste it into the address bar, then click Go or hit Enter.

## UNWANTED DOWNLOADS

**Problem**

You open a Web page and see a message stating that you must download a program to properly view a site.

**Remedy**

Think before you download this kind of program. First, if you do it at school you may be violating download policies. Second, if it happens at home you can quickly clutter your hard drive with programs you don't need. Third, some of these programs actually upload information about your Internet surfing habits to commercial businesses. Finally, this can be a way that a virus or other harmful program can be introduced into your computer. So, you may miss out on an occasional extraordinary site, but it's worth it in order to avoid more serious problems. As you increase your Internet use, you may want to talk with your school's technician to find out which of these programs are OK for downloading.

## CHAPTER 3

# Beyond the Basics

N ow that you have Internet basics under your belt, you may be
perfectly content to stick with what you know, and that's
great. However, if you find yourself thinking, "There must be
another way to get where I want to be on the Internet," you're
in the right place. This chapter explains how to circumvent some limita-
tions of certain browsers, work with more than one Internet window
simultaneously, organize your favorite Web sites and pages, and
conduct your own searches on the Internet.

# USING MULTIPLE BROWSERS

Even after you've established a means for connecting to the Internet and have selected an ISP, there may be times when you choose to use one browser over another. It's not uncommon to find several different browser programs preinstalled on a computer's hard drive, for instance, Internet Explorer, Netscape, and AOL.

Accessing the Internet from multiple computer systems or locations may actually create a need to use more than one browser. For example, if you have a DSL connection, you might use Internet Explorer as the default browser. However, when traveling, DSL may not be available. A paid account for a national ISP such as AOL, on the other hand, enables you to make a toll-free dial-up connection almost everywhere you go.

Another reason to use multiple browsers is that some Web sites work better with one browser than with another. For example, a site page that shows lots of white space and requires considerable scrolling to see everything on the page when viewed in Netscape may look just fine in Internet Explorer. The opposite also happens; a page that looks funny in Internet Explorer will be quite readable in Netscape. How will you know when the browser makes a difference?

Often, the site's home page will clearly state "This site best viewed using …" and will name the preferred browser or browsers. Other times, you'll find out through trial and error. In any event, if the spacing on a page doesn't seem to make sense, or if the graphics aren't clear, try switching browsers. If you're using a DSL or other high-speed connection and your computer is Internet-connected whenever it's on, simply close the browser you're currently using and double-click on the icon for the browser you'd like to open. Then cut and paste the URL of the page you're visiting into the address bar. Of course, to use AOL or another subscription service, you must have a paid account to use the proprietary browser.

Speaking of AOL, many users mistakenly think their ability to access or use certain sites is limited because they use AOL (some sites state "This feature not available to AOL users"). That may be true if you try to go through AOL's Internet browser, but you have an alternative. Once you've signed on and made your online connection, minimize the AOL browser window so that you can see your Desktop. You still have the Internet connection established and can open Internet Explorer or Netscape and use one of these browsers to access sites. If you want to return to AOL, simply click on the AOL icon in the menu bar at the bottom of your screen.

# USING MULTIPLE WINDOWS

Sometimes you may want to have more than one Internet site open at once. Perhaps you want to flip back and forth to compare content, or you're using information from one site to complete an online form on another. It's more efficient to do this using additional windows than using the Back and Forward tools.

Opening a second window is easy (Figure 1). Click on File on the menu bar, scroll to New, and click on Window. Depending on your browser, the new window will either display your home page or a duplicate of the site you had open when you executed the new-window command. Once you've opened another window, you can enter a new URL as usual.

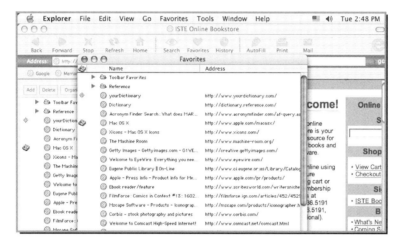

FIGURE 1. Opening a new window.

Moving back and forth between your browser and other types of open windows is also easy (Figure 2). To keep your desktop clean, minimize each when you're not looking at it. In Windows, minimized windows appear in the menu bar at the bottom of your screen. The small icon at the left of each title tells you what kind of file each is (such as Word or Internet Explorer). To move back and forth between Internet files, click on the buttons labeled with the Internet Explorer icon. If you have numerous windows open, minimized items will appear in a pop-up list (Figure 2). In Mac OS X, minimized sites are stored to the right end of your dock. Simply click on the image to return the page or file to your desktop.

You can also use these buttons to move between Internet files and other documents, such as a word processing file. In Figure 2, a Word document has been minimized along with several Web pages. To switch to the word-processing document, click once on that button.

Word document      Explorer Web pages

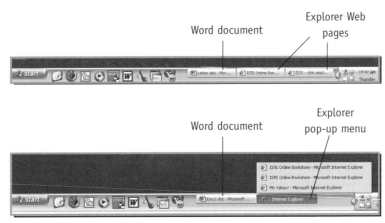

Word document      Explorer pop-up menu

FIGURE 2. At top are separate buttons for each minimized item—two buttons for open Internet Explorer pages and one for a Word document. Open a window by clicking on its button. At bottom, the Explorer pages appear in a list.

You can "tile" windows on the screen so that you can see two or more simultaneously. On Mac running OS X, simply press F9. Press again to return to your previous view. To access the Tile Windows command on the PC, point your cursor at the gray area to the right of the menu bar at the bottom of your screen (Figure 3). Right-click once, scroll to either Tile Windows Horizontally or Tile Windows Vertically, and click again. Every currently open file will be displayed. To return to viewing just one window, right-click in the gray area again and select the Undo Tile option that appears.

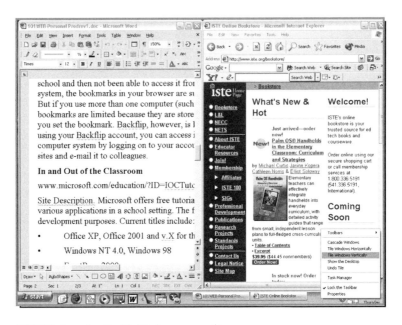

FIGURE 3. Accessing the Tile Windows commands.

Although tiling can be useful, most people seem to prefer the method shown in Figure 2 because the tiled images quickly become too small to read easily and more scrolling is required to see everything on a page.

## ORGANIZING YOUR FAVORITES

After a while, you may find you have added so many bookmarks that your list of favorite Web sites and pages is quite lengthy and you can't remember what a particular bookmark is or why you saved it! To avoid confusion, you can set up file folders for your favorites, just like you set up folders for word processing and other files you want to keep. To access the Favorites window in Internet Explorer, click on the Favorites button on the main toolbar or click on the Favorites tab, then select Organize (Figure 4). In Netscape, go to Bookmarks, then Organize Bookmarks. Figure 5 shows the Favorites window in Internet Explorer.

FIGURE 4. From the Favorites panel, click on the Organize button, then choose Open Favorites Window.

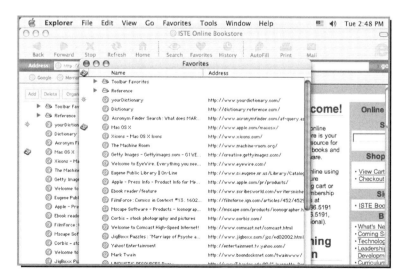

FIGURE 5. Favorites window.

### Creating a New Folder

Open your Favorites panel, then position your cursor over the Organize button, and click once again. Select New Folder (Figure 4). A new folder then appears in the list. Type a name for the folder and press the Enter key.

### To Move a Favorite

To move a favorite Web site or page into a folder, or from one folder to another, open the folder you want to move it to by clicking on the folder. Then select and drag the site or page into the folder. The short black line shows where the item will appear. This feature makes it easy to organize your favorites in any order you like. If the site or page is already in a folder, you will need to click on the name of that folder to open it and see what's currently stored within the folder.

### To Delete a Favorite

You may find that you no longer want to have a site included in your list of favorites. To delete a site, click on the one you want to delete until it's highlighted (don't click too fast or it will launch the page). Then click once on the Delete button in the pop-up menu or the Delete button at the top of the list (Figure 6). The site is gone from the list.

FIGURE 6. This pop-up menu makes it easy to manage your list of favorites.

### Renaming a Favorite

Often when adding a site to your list of favorites, the name that appears on the list makes little or no sense to you. You can easily rename a favorite site, giving it a name that's more meaningful and easier to find later. Click on the name you want to change to highlight it (don't click too fast or it will launch the page), then select Rename or Edit Name, depending on your browser (Figure 6). Now you can type the new name and press the Enter key. With some browsers, you can highlight the name and type in a new name (Figure 7).

FIGURE 7. Rename Web sites so they're understandable to you.

## To Close the Organize Box

When you're finished organizing your favorite sites and pages, click once on the Favorites button or the Favorites tab.

# CONDUCTING SUCCESSFUL SEARCHES

Many Internet users love to surf the Web, moving from site to site looking for interesting pages. If you happen to have a lot of time on your hands and don't need to find something specific quickly, it can be fun to poke around and see what you come up with. However, most of us can't afford to spend that kind of time on the off chance we might find something interesting. Using a Web directory or a search engine can point you in the right direction and ensure that your time online is well spent.

---

**VOCABULARY TERMS**

**search engine**
A program that searches files for specified keywords and produces a list of files containing the keywords. Although the term refers to this type of program, people generally use the term to refer to such Web sites as Google, Alta Vista, or Excite, which use such programs to search for files on the World Wide Web.

**Web directory**
A list of categories and subcategories you can browse to find Web sites. It's most helpful when you're looking for general information.

---

## Web Directories

Some popular Web directories include WebCrawler (**www.webcrawler.com/info.wbcrwl/**) and Yahoo! (**www.yahoo.com**). Figure 8 shows a directory listing from Yahoo! To use a directory, simply choose a category and click on it to see the subcategories listed within. You can trace the categories and subcategories you've looked at by referring to the bar near the top of the screen, which shows the title of each category and subcategory you've accessed (Figure 9). A Web directory can be a useful tool when you're interested in a general topic but aren't exactly sure what you're looking for. For instance, you may want to look at some examples of school Web sites but don't have particular schools in mind. Yahoo!'s Web directory allows you to go to an area called Schools where you can select grade levels, then states where the schools are located, then a list of schools that have Web sites in each state.

FIGURE 8. Web directory.

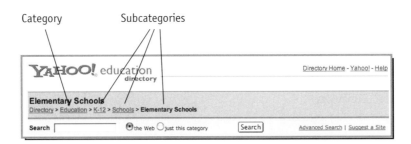

FIGURE 9. Tracing the steps taken in a search using a Web directory.

## Search Engines

When you need to find something specific, such as an online article, it's best to use a search engine. Search engines search an index of Web pages looking for keywords you've entered in a text box. Each search engine uses its own index, so you'll find different results using different engines.

Some of the more popular search engines include Google (**www.google.com**), Alta Vista (**www.altavista.com**), and Lycos (**www.lycos.com**). Figure 10 shows a search results page for a search done by Google.

Results are shown as hyperlinks. Click on the title to access the Web site.

Advanced Search features may be accessed here to improve your searching techniques.

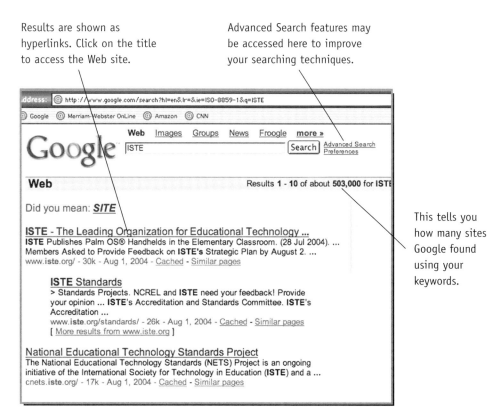

This tells you how many sites Google found using your keywords.

FIGURE 10. Google search results page.

Clustering search engines show results grouped by theme. Popular clustering search engines include Vivisimo (**www.vivisimo.com**) and Kartoo (**www.kartoo.com**). Figure 11 shows a search results page for a search done using Kartoo.

Searching for sites can be frustrating if you simply rely on using keywords without knowing a few tricks to use along the way. Bernie Dodge, Ph.D., is a professor of educational technology at San Diego State University. He works with educators who are learning to use the Internet and has developed what he calls Four NETS for Better Searching (here, NETS is an acronym for the four steps you take when searching and should not be confused with the ISTE-sponsored NETS project, which

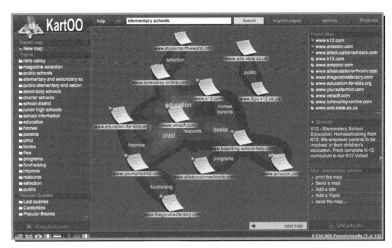

FIGURE 11. Kartoo search results page.

focuses on student, teacher, and administrator technology standards). These four tips are some of the best around, and Professor Dodge has graciously agreed to have them listed here for you. They're based on the Google search engine.

1. **Start Narrow:** Search engines allow you to identify words you want included in your search, as well as words you don't want to include. For example, click on the Advanced Search option of Google, where you can define keywords in the following categories:

   - with **all** the words

   - with **any** of the words

   - **without** the words

   This is helpful when conducting a search for a particular person, place, or thing that may share its name with multiple others. If you want to find Washington Elementary School in a city in Florida rather than every Washington Elementary School across the country, you can use the name of the city and state to narrow the search.

2. **Find Exact Phrases:** When you enter multiple keywords, the results will list every site in the search engine's database with the words together or individually. Thus, if you search using the keywords *elementary school,* you'll get all occurrences of the words collectively and individually. That may be OK until you start finding results that quote Sherlock Holmes ("Elementary, my dear Watson") rather than sites related to elementary schools. Search engines allow you to indicate that you want only sites that include the **exact phrase** you're using as keywords.

3. **Trim Back the URL:** You may find an interesting site in a search that has a long URL. For example, suppose you've discovered a resource for research at

http://www.iste.org/research/caret.html. You may think the site could offer additional information elsewhere. Trim the URL by leaving off the last portion after the final backslash: http://www.iste.org/research/. Trim it once again to http://www.iste.org. This technique can also work when you receive a message that a particular page is no longer available. Trimming the URL may help you find the page at a new location within the site.

4. Look for Similar Pages: Look at Figure 10. Each Web site listed in Results has a hyperlink called Similar Pages. By clicking on this link, you can access additional pages Google identifies as having content much like the page listed.

You can read more about the Four NETS for Better Searching and run through some search practice exercises by visiting http://webquest.sdsu.edu/searching/fournets.htm. Once you're comfortable using the advanced search options with Google, explore the advanced options with another search engine, such as Alta Vista or Lycos.

## CHAPTER 4

# Internet Security

The Internet offers a wide array of useful resources. Unfortunately, accessing them can make your computer vulnerable to a host of problems. You've probably heard of computer viruses, worms, and Trojan Horses, all of which can of wreaking havoc if they get on your system. In the old days, viruses were spread primarily through infected floppies or e-mail attachments, but now they can gain access to your system in a variety of ways, including the Internet.

Malicious programs can lurk anywhere online—in an interactive Web application, a Java applet, or a poisoned cookie. Automated programs roam the Internet looking for vulnerable systems to attack and personal information to steal. Once the damage to your system is done, it's difficult to set things right; sometimes even a computer technician can't save your infected files or corrupted data.

In this chapter, the most common security threats are defined, along with steps you can take to avoid them so that you can surf safely.

# SAFE SURFING

While the information technology (IT) team at your school or district works to protect your network's security, team members rely on the support of users who practice "safe surfing." At work, being aware of security threats helps maintain the integrity of your system and the confidentiality of your data. At home, you're likely on your own, so awareness is even more essential.

Threats can be broken down into three major categories, each with its own particular set of countermeasures:

| THREAT | COUNTERMEASURE |
|---|---|
| malware | antivirus programs |
| spyware | anti-spyware program |
| spoofs | security patches and firewalls |

# MALWARE

Malware is malicious software designed to damage computer files or disrupt system and network operations. Here are definitions of the most common types.

**virus:** Just like its disease-causing counterpart in nature, a virus is a piece of computer code that is able to replicate itself once it's found a host (your computer). A virus can be downloaded without your knowledge and execute or run itself without your permission. Because it copies itself over and over, even the simplest virus can cause problems. Viruses can quickly use up a computer's available memory, making the system inoperable. Viruses can also carry a "payload"—malicious code that corrupts and destroys crucial files on your computer. While Windows computers continue to be the predominant target of virus writers, Unix/Linux and Macintosh computers aren't immune.

**worm:** A worm, like a virus, can replicate rapidly, bringing a computer system to a standstill by using up available memory. Unlike a virus, a worm doesn't hide in, or attach itself to, another file or program; it's a stand-alone program that roams networks autonomously, bogging down computers, destroying files, stealing passwords and credit card numbers, and opening back doors.

---

**VOCABULARY TERM**

**malware**
A generic term for malicious software. Programs of this type are intentionally designed to damage computer files or disrupt normal system and network operations.

---

## VOCABULARY TERMS

**virus**

A piece of computer code that can replicate itself once it has found a host (your computer). A virus can be downloaded without your knowledge and execute or run itself without your permission.

**worm**

A computer program that roams networks autonomously, bogging computers down by using up available memory, destroying files, stealing passwords and credit card numbers, and opening backdoors on infected systems.

**Trojan Horse**

Named after the gift horse of Trojan War fame, this is malware that masquerades as a free game or useful utility program. Once it is downloaded onto your computer, however, it can unleash a worm or keylogger or open a backdoor into your system.

**Trojan horse:** Named after the gift horse of Trojan War fame, this malware masquerades as a free game or useful utility program. Once it's downloaded onto your computer, it can unleash a worm or keylogger, or open a back door into your system.

**back door:** A program that runs secretly on a computer, opening a hole in its security that allows outsiders access to the system. A back door typically opens a connection to the Internet and broadcasts a message detectable by "port scanners" that hackers use to find vulnerable computers. Once the hacker accesses your system through the back door, he can steal personal information, corrupt data, or commandeer your computer and use it with other compromised computers to create a "zombie network." Zombie networks have been used to launch denial-of-service attacks on Web sites and flood e-mail servers with virus-laden or spoofed e-mails.

**keylogger:** This is another program that runs secretly on a computer, tracking every keystroke a user makes and sending that information back to the program's creator. Keyloggers are most often used to steal credit card numbers, passwords, or other personal information.

How can you protect yourself from these virtual contagions? While there's no surefire way to immunize your system from every possible attack, here are steps you can take to make infection from malware much less likely.

1. **Purchase antivirus software.** Numerous high-quality antivirus programs are available to protect against viruses, worms, and Trojan horses. Some of them are even free. Norton Antivirus and McAfee VirusScan are the two most popular choices, but other good choices include PC-Cillin Internet Security, Panda

Antivirus, BitDefender, and AVG Antivirus. While many free antivirus programs are advertised on the Internet, be wary: in the past, several infamous Trojan horses have masqueraded as free antivirus programs. Talk with your IT team to learn what programs they recommend.

2. **Regularly update your antivirus software.** This can't be emphasized too strongly. An out-of-date antivirus program is just as dangerous as *no* antivirus protection. With new viruses and variants of old viruses released every day, it's imperative that your program's virus definitions be updated as often as possible. Most good antivirus programs automate this process. When you purchase the software, you also purchase a subscription to virus definition updates. The program will automatically search for new definitions every time you connect to the Internet (or every few hours if your computer is always connected). If new definitions are found, they are downloaded and added to your program's "hit list" of malicious code to watch out for. This subscription is limited to a specific length of time, usually a year. To continue to receive updates, you need to renew your subscription.

3. **Use your antivirus software.** This may seem obvious, but many people aren't using their antivirus program effectively. Be sure your program is configured to automatically scan any file before it's opened or executed. This is typically the default setting for the program. You should also schedule regular full-system scans—scans of every file on your hard drive—to check for malware that may have snuck in unannounced.

4. **Be careful with e-mail.** Special care should be taken with e-mail and e-mail attachments, still the most common vehicle for malware transmission. Good antivirus programs will automatically scan e-mails before downloading them, since viruses can hide in an image or script embedded in the message itself (not just in an attachment). Make sure this feature is turned on.

5. **Be careful with Internet downloads.** Take special care with any program you download from the Internet. Legitimate software programs are "signed." This means the distributor has verified the safety of the download and can be held responsible for any problems. Unsigned downloads may be malware, so don't

---

**VOCABULARY TERMS**

**back door**
A program that runs secretly on a computer, opening a hole in its security that allows outsiders access to the system.

**keylogger**
A program that runs secretly on a computer, tracking every keystroke that a user makes and sending that information back to its creator. Keyloggers are most often used to steal credit card numbers, passwords, or other personal information.

accept them! Ask your IT team how to configure your Internet browser so that it won't accept any unsigned downloads. When you do download a program, carefully read the software-use policy or agreement before installing it. Free programs such as screensavers, media plug-ins, and file-sharing utilities are frequently bundled with programs that may be adware or spyware, so be sure you aren't agreeing to install any programs you don't want.

# SPYWARE

Spyware is software that gathers data about you and the way you use your computer, usually for commercial purposes. Spyware has quickly come to rival viruses and spam e-mails as a major problem for Internet users.

Spyware comes in many forms, invading your computer without your knowledge or consent. Spyware can arrive attached to programs you've downloaded. It can also come in the form of "tracking cookies" uploaded to your computer when you visit a particular Web site. Once on your computer, the spyware compromises your privacy by gathering data (such as what Web sites you visit or what you buy online) and, through your Internet connection, transmitting the data back to the Web site's originator. You may not be aware at first that spyware is running on your computer. However, as spyware accumulates on your hard drive, your system will start to bog down.

Like any other program, spyware runs by using your computer's memory. It also uses up some of your Internet bandwidth to communicate with its maker. If you have these programs running in the background, your computer may lack the system resources to run programs you *want* to run, and your Internet connection will slow to a crawl. Poorly written spyware can even crash your system.

While most spyware targets users with advertisements for specific products and services (an alternative name is **adware**), some varieties truly earn malware status. The most common are **browser hijackers**—spyware programs that change your Internet browser settings. Browser hijackers change your home page without your consent and typically add links to other sites (often pornographic in nature) to your list of Bookmarks or Favorites. This is not just a nuisance issue: a few cases have been reported of employees losing their jobs because of Web links found on their

---

**VOCABULARY TERM**

**spyware**
Software that gathers data about you and the way you use your computer, usually for commercial purposes. Often referred to as adware.

**VOCABULARY TERM**

**browser hijackers**
Spyware programs that change your Internet browser settings, such as your home page or bookmark list, without your consent.

computer that may have been placed there by hijackers. Sometimes a hijack program will deny you access to antivirus and anti-spyware Web sites, or even disable the antivirus software on your computer.

Browser hijackers get onto your computer just like other spyware programs. They can be bundled together with free utility programs and games, so be sure to read the software use policy carefully before installing anything you download from the Internet. Another popular technique is the pop-up download, in which a small window pops up on your screen when you visit a particular site, informing you that you need to download a program to "optimize" your browser or view all of the content on that site. These messages are deceptively worded to encourage you to select "Yes" and agree to the download; they often look and sound like the update reminders from legitimate programs already on your computer, so read carefully!

Finally, and most alarmingly, there is the "drive-by download," in which the hijacker is downloaded invisibly when you visit a site or read an HTML e-mail message. The first clue that your browser has been hijacked may come when you notice your home page has suddenly changed, or when you find yourself being redirected to question-able sites whenever you try to navigate away from the page you're viewing.

Among the growing number of anti-spyware programs available for purchase or free download, the most popular are Ad-aware and Spybot Search and Destroy (other titles include SpywareBlaster and SpywareGuide's X-Blaster). Also, antivirus programs now often provide spyware protection. Because of the numerous forms spyware can take, it's a good idea to have more than one anti-spyware solution.

Remember that downloading and installing anti-spyware software isn't enough: you need to update the spyware definitions daily or weekly (just as you do with your antivirus program) and scan your system regularly. It's also crucial that you download and install any security patches and updates available for your system.

# SPOOFING

Spoofing is a technique used by hackers to gain unauthorized access to a computer or network share. Spoofing involves the crafting of an e-mail message or Web site that appears to be coming from a trusted source—a computer or software manufacturer, a bank or credit card company, your Internet service provider, and so forth. Spoofed messages will often direct the user to download a patch or update (launching a backdoor or keylogger instead), or visit an official-looking Web site where the same kind of malware awaits. Sometimes, the message will ask for passwords and other personal information that can be used to gain direct access to the user's computer or network accounts.

Spoofing works because the author of the message or Web site has stolen the IP address (the number that uniquely identifies a computer connected to the Internet) of the trusted source and has altered the packets of information coming from his own machine so that it appears they are coming from that source. In other words, the message or site appears to be coming from a Microsoft or Citibank server rather than Hank Hacker's computer. Spoofed e-mails can be subtly persuasive or officious and intimidating and are difficult for less experienced users to resist. Recently, spoofed messages have been created that require no action at all from the user; instead, a script embedded in the message itself launches the malicious program once the user views it.

Whether or not they're spoofing, hackers find a way to exploit vulnerabilities in new software almost immediately, then they post their discoveries on Web sites for others to enjoy and use. These security holes then become the targets of viruses, worms, and malware of every description. The Windows operating system and such Microsoft programs as Internet Explorer and Outlook Express have been notoriously vulnerable to such attacks. Hackers have targeted Windows primarily because it's the predominant operating system throughout the world, not because the Macintosh OS or Unix/Linux is invulnerable to attack.

---

**VOCABULARY TERM**

**Spoofing**
A technique used by hackers to gain unauthorized access to a computer or network share by imitating a trusted source in an e-mail message or on a Web site.

---

# HOW TO PROTECT YOURSELF

Start by making sure you always download and install all critical security updates for your operating system and software. This update process has been automated for Windows and Macintosh computers. So as long as you have your computer configured to automatically accept all critical updates (the default setting), you'll be closing any security holes as soon as patches are available. One caveat: because some security updates have caused problems for network administrators, your IT team may want to research compatibility issues before you install updates.

**Firewalls** prevent unauthorized access to your system by filtering every packet of information coming in from or going out to the Internet, then blocking traffic that doesn't meet its security criteria. Firewalls can be built into hardware (such as network routers and gateways) or software (programs from Norton, McAfee, ZoneAlarm, Sygate, and many others). Your school or district is almost certainly using firewalls to protect the network from attack. If you also have a personal firewall installed on your work computer, check with IT personnel to make sure it's properly configured and isn't interfering with network security or your ability to use the Web.

---

**VOCABULARY TERM**

**firewall**

Hardware or software that protects a computer system from intrusion. It prevents unauthorized access by filtering every packet of information coming in from or going out to the Internet and blocking any traffic that does not meet its security criteria.

---

# IF YOU FIND YOURSELF IN TROUBLE

Keeping up-to-date on all the potential vulnerabilities of computers and networks is a full-time job for security experts and not something you should expect to handle yourself. If you suspect that your computer has fallen prey to any of the attacks described in this section, contact your IT team immediately and describe the problem to the experts. If your system has been compromised by a hacker, it's quite likely that other computers on your network have also been compromised. Resolving security intrusions and repairing the damage they can cause is a job for trained network technicians.

Your IT team is your first stop if your school or office computer becomes infected. If you experience a problem on your home computer, several nonprofit Web sites offer free advice and information to help you get out of sticky situations, such as a hijacked browser home page or a virus infection. Sometimes entering a description of the problem in a search engine will direct you to a solution. One helpful site is Tech Support Guy (**www.techguy.org**). This site is run by knowledgeable volunteers and is supported by donations, usually from grateful Internet surfers who have been helped out of jams. Once you've registered, you can post your problem to a forum. Registration is free.

# SCREENSHOT CREDITS

## PART 1. Directory of Internet Sites

### Curriculum
Page 9: By permission of Achieve.org.
Page 10: By permission of the Clearinghouse on Reading, English, and Communication/Indiana University School of Education.
Page 11: By permission of Mid-continent Research for Education and Learning.
Page 13: By permission of Educational REALMS.
Page 15: By permission of International Reading Association.
Page 16: By permission of MarcoPolo.
Page 17: By permission of National Council for the Social Studies.
Page 18: By permission of National Council of Teachers of English.
Page 19: © 2005 by the National Council of Teachers of Mathematics. Used with permission. All rights reserved.
Page 20: © 2005 by the National Science Teachers Association. All rights reserved.
Page 22: By permission of Social Studies Development Center.

### Data-Driven Decision Making
Page 28: By permission of National Center for Research on Evaluation, Standards, and Student Testing.
Page 29: By permission of National Center on Educational Outcomes.
Page 30: By permission of School Information Partnership.
Page 32: By permission of American Youth Policy Forum, Research and Evaluation.
Page 33: By permission of North Central Regional Educational Laboratory.

### Finance
Page 37: By permission of Education Commission of the States: Finance.
Page 38: By permission of Education Finance Database.
Page 41: By permission of Grants and Contests.
Page 42: By permission of Mid-continent Research for Education and Learning.
Page 43: By permission of School Finance Project.
Page 44: © 2005 by Scholastic Inc. All rights reserved. Reprinted with permission.
Page 45: By permission of Courtesy of Donna Fernandez and SchoolGrants.org.

### General
Page 49: AOL@SCHOOL is a registered trademark of America Online, Inc. Used with permission.
Page 50: Used with permission of Clearinghouse on Educational Policy and Management, College of Education, University of Oregon.
Page 51: By permission of e-Lead is a partnership of the Laboratory for Student Success at Temple Univeristy and the Institute for Educational Leadership.
Page 53: By permission of School Administrators Center.
Page 54: Reprinted by permission. © 2004 Teachnology, Inc.

### Instruction
Page 59: By permission of About Learning.
Page 60: Big6™ Skills for Information Problem Solving © 1987. Michael B. Eisenberg & Robert E. Berkowitz.
Page 61: By permission of Center for Applied Research and Educational Improvement, College of Education and Human Development, University of Minnesota.
Page 62: © 2005 SBC Knowledge Ventures, L.P. All rights reserved.
Page 63: By permission of Area Education Agency 267, Cedar Falls, Iowa; Nancy Lockett, author.
Page 64: By permission of Landmarks for Schools and David Warlick.
Page 65: By permission of The Principals' Partnership.
Page 66: By permission of NCRTEC.
Page 67: By permission of the Web site of the American Library Association.

### Personal Productivity
Page 71: Product screenshot reprinted with permission from Adobe Systems Incorporated.
Page 73: By permission of In and Out of the Classroom.
Page 75: By permission of Courtesy of the Software995 Corporation.

### Professional Development
Page 79: By permission of Career-Long Teacher Development: Policies That Make Sense.
Page 81: © 2005 The George Lucas Educational Foundation. All rights reserved. Printed with permission.
Page 82: By permission of The Finance Project. All rights reserved.
Page 83: By permission of Mid-continent Research for Education and Learning.
Page 84: By permission of North Central Regional Educational Laboratory.

### Professional Organizations
Page 87: Reprinted with permission of the American Association of School Administrators.
Page 88: By permission of the Association for Supervision and Curriculum Development.
Page 90: By permission of the National Association of Elementary School Principals.
Page 92: By permission of the National Middle School Association.
Page 93: By permission of the National Staff Development Council.

### Professional Reading
Page 97: By permission of ASCD's SmartBrief.
Page 98: By permission of The Doyle Report.
Page 99: By permission of Ed Week Update.

Page 101: By permission of Public Education
Network.
Page 102: © Phi Delta Kappa International, Inc.
Page 103: By permission of Reading Online.
Page 104: © 2005 by Scholastic Inc. All rights
reserved. Reprinted with permission. Scholastic
Administr@tor is a registered trademark of
Scholastic Inc.
Page 105: By permission of School Administrator.
Page 106: By permission of Technology and
Learning Magazine.
Page 107: By permission of Today's School.

## Research Institutes and Education Centers
Page 111: By permission of Annenberg Institute
for School Reform.
Page 113: By permission of The Education Alliance
at Brown University.
Page 115: By permission of Laboratory for Student
Success: The Mid-Atlantic Regional Educational
Laboratory.
Page 116: By permission of Mid-continent Research
for Education and Learning.
Page 117: By permission of North Central Regional
Educational Laboratory.
Page 119: By permission of Pacific Resources
for Education and Learning.
Page 120: By permission of RAND Education.
Page 121: By permission of Southeast Regional
Vision for Education.
Page 122: By permission of Southwest Educational
Development Laboratory.
Page 123: By permission of WestEd.

## Social and Legal Issues
Page 127: By permission of Center for
the Prevention of School Violence.
Page 130: By permission of NEA Crisis
Communications Guide & Toolkit.

## Technology Use
Page 134: Created for the Consortium for School
Networking by Driven by Design.
Page 135: By permission of Educator's Reference
Desk: Educational Technology.
Page 136: By permission of Network of Regional
Technology in Education Consortia.
Page 138: By permission of Courtesy Pew Internet
& American Life Project.
Page 139: By permission of Technology Information
Center for Administrative Leadership.

## PART 2. Internet Survival Skills

Internet Browser and Windows desktop screenshots
reprinted by permission from Microsoft
Corporation.
Page 172: © 2005 Yahoo! Inc. Reprinted with permission. YAHOO! and the YAHOO! logo are
trademarks of Yahoo! Inc.
Page 173: © 2005 Google Inc. Reprinted with permission.
Page 174: © 2005 Kartoo. Reprinted with permission.

# Correlation to NETS•A

**P**rincipals who are engaged in coursework for credentialing or professional growth may be required to develop and implement action plans based on the National Educational Technology Standards for Administrators (NETS•A). Or, as part of their own evaluation process, principals may be asked to develop a professional growth plan, including work in the area of instructional technology.

Every site listed in part 1, "Directory of Internet Sites," provides resources and materials that can help you develop and fulfill these professional growth plans, including implementation of one or more of the NETS•A and their performance indicators.

The full text of these standards and performance indicators follows, along with a table for each section of the directory. Next to each Web site name and URL is a matrix that indicates which of the NETS•A standards are related to the primary areas of emphasis in that site.

# NATIONAL EDUCATIONAL TECHNOLOGY STANDARDS FOR ADMINISTRATORS (NETS•A)

All school administrators should be prepared to meet the following standards and performance indicators. These standards are a national consensus among educational stakeholders regarding what best indicates effective school leadership for comprehensive and appropriate use of technology in schools.

## I. Leadership and Vision

Educational leaders inspire a shared vision for comprehensive integration of technology and foster an environment and culture conducive to the realization of that vision. Educational leaders:

  A. facilitate the shared development by all stakeholders of a vision for technology use and widely communicate that vision.

  B. maintain an inclusive and cohesive process to develop, implement, and monitor a dynamic, long-range, and systemic technology plan to achieve the vision.

  C. foster and nurture a culture of responsible risk-taking and advocate policies promoting continuous innovation with technology.

  D. use data in making leadership decisions.

  E. advocate for research-based effective practices in use of technology.

  F. advocate, on the state and national levels, for policies, programs, and funding opportunities that support implementation of the district technology plan.

## II. Learning and Teaching

Educational leaders ensure that curricular design, instructional strategies, and learning environments integrate appropriate technologies to maximize learning and teaching. Educational leaders:

  A. identify, use, evaluate, and promote appropriate technologies to enhance and support instruction and standards-based curriculum leading to high levels of student achievement.

  B. facilitate and support collaborative technology-enriched learning environments conducive to innovation for improved learning.

  C. provide for learner-centered environments that use technology to meet the individual and diverse needs of learners.

  D. facilitate the use of technologies to support and enhance instructional methods that develop higher-level thinking, decision-making, and problem-solving skills.

  E. provide for and ensure that faculty and staff take advantage of quality professional learning opportunities for improved learning and teaching with technology.

## III. Productivity and Professional Practice

Educational leaders apply technology to enhance their professional practice and to increase their own productivity and that of others. Educational leaders:

A. model the routine, intentional, and effective use of technology.

B. employ technology for communication and collaboration among colleagues, staff, parents, students, and the larger community.

C. create and participate in learning communities that stimulate, nurture, and support faculty and staff in using technology for improved productivity.

D. engage in sustained, job-related professional learning using technology resources.

E. maintain awareness of emerging technologies and their potential uses in education.

F. use technology to advance organizational improvement.

## IV. Support, Management, and Operations

Educational leaders ensure the integration of technology to support productive systems for learning and administration. Educational leaders:

A. develop, implement, and monitor policies and guidelines to ensure compatibility of technologies.

B. implement and use integrated technology-based management and operations systems.

C. allocate financial and human resources to ensure complete and sustained implementation of the technology plan.

D. integrate strategic plans, technology plans, and other improvement plans and policies to align efforts and leverage resources.

E. implement procedures to drive continuous improvements of technology systems and to support technology replacement cycles.

## V. Assessment and Evaluation

Educational leaders use technology to plan and implement comprehensive systems of effective assessment and evaluation. Educational leaders:

A. use multiple methods to assess and evaluate appropriate uses of technology resources for learning, communication, and productivity.

B. use technology to collect and analyze data, interpret results, and communicate findings to improve instructional practice and student learning.

C. assess staff knowledge, skills, and performance in using technology and use results to facilitate quality professional development and to inform personnel decisions.

D. use technology to assess, evaluate, and manage administrative and operational systems.

## VI. Social, Legal, and Ethical Issues

Educational leaders understand the social, legal, and ethical issues related to technology and model responsible decision-making related to these issues. Educational leaders:

A. ensure equity of access to technology resources that enable and empower all learners and educators.

**B.** identify, communicate, model, and enforce social, legal, and ethical practices to promote responsible use of technology.

**C.** promote and enforce privacy, security, and online safety related to the use of technology.

**D.** promote and enforce environmentally safe and healthy practices in the use of technology.

**E.** participate in the development of policies that clearly enforce copyright law and assign ownership of intellectual property developed with district resources.

*This material was originally produced as a project of the Technology Standards for School Administrators Collaborative.*

# NETS•A CORRELATION MATRIX: CURRICULUM

| NAME OF SITE/INTERNET ADDRESS | STANDARDS | | | | | |
|---|---|---|---|---|---|---|
| | I. LEADERSHIP AND VISION | II. LEARNING AND TEACHING | III. PRODUCTIVITY AND PROFESSIONAL PRACTICE | IV. SUPPORT, MANAGEMENT, AND OPERATIONS | V. ASSESSMENT AND EVALUATION | VI. SOCIAL, LEGAL, AND ETHICAL ISSUES |
| Achieve.org<br>www.achieve.org/achieve.nsf/home?openform | | ▓ | | | ▓ | |
| Clearinghouse on Reading, English, & Communication<br>reading.indiana.edu | | ▓ | | | | |
| Content Knowledge, Third Edition<br>www.mcrel.org/standards-benchmarks/ | | ▓ | | | | |
| Early Childhood and Parenting Collaborative<br>ecap.crc.uiuc.edu/info/ | ▓ | ▓ | | | | |
| Educational REALMS<br>www.stemworks.org/realmshomepage.html | | ▓ | | | | |
| Federal Resources for Educational Excellence (FREE)<br>www.ed.gov/free/ | | ▓ | | | | |
| International Reading Association (IRA)<br>www.reading.org | | ▓ | | | ▓ | |
| MarcoPolo<br>www.marcopolo-education.org | | ▓ | | | | |
| National Council for the Social Studies (NCSS)<br>www.ncss.org or www.socialstudies.org | | ▓ | | | | |
| National Council of Teachers of English (NCTE)<br>www.ncte.org | | ▓ | | | | |
| National Council of Teachers of Mathematics (NCTM)<br>www.nctm.org | | ▓ | | | | |
| National Science Teachers Association (NSTA)<br>www.nsta.org/administrators | | ▓ | | | | |
| No Child Left Behind<br>www.ed.gov/nclb/landing.jhtml?src=pb | | ▓ | | | ▓ | ▓ |
| Social Studies Development Center<br>www.indiana.edu/%7Essdc/ssdc.htm | | ▓ | | | | |
| Standards and Accountability<br>www.publicengagement.com/resources/standards/ | | ▓ | | | ▓ | |

# NETS•A CORRELATION MATRIX: DATA-DRIVEN DECISION MAKING

| NAME OF SITE/INTERNET ADDRESS | STANDARDS | | | | | |
|---|---|---|---|---|---|---|
| | I. LEADERSHIP AND VISION | II. LEARNING AND TEACHING | III. PRODUCTIVITY AND PROFESSIONAL PRACTICE | IV. SUPPORT, MANAGEMENT, AND OPERATIONS | V. ASSESSMENT AND EVALUATION | VI. SOCIAL, LEGAL, AND ETHICAL ISSUES |
| National Assessment Governing Board (NAGB) **www.nagb.org** | | | | | ▨ | |
| National Center for Research on Evaluation, Standards, and Student Testing (CRESST) **www.cse.ucla.edu** | | | | | ▨ | |
| National Center on Educational Outcomes (NCEO) **education.umn.edu/nceo/** | | | | | ▨ | ▨ |
| School Information Partnership **www.schoolresults.org** | | | | | ▨ | ▨ |
| Student Data Handbook for Elementary, Secondary, and Early Childhood Education **nces.ed.gov/pubsearch/ pubsinfo.asp?pubid=2000343r** | | | | | ▨ | |
| Thinking About Tests and Testing: A Short Primer in "Assessment Literacy" **www.aypf.org/subcats/repubs.htm** | | | | | ▨ | |
| The ToolBelt **www.ncrel.org/toolbelt/** | | | | | ▨ | |

# NETS•A CORRELATION MATRIX: FINANCE

| NAME OF SITE/INTERNET ADDRESS | STANDARDS | | | | | |
|---|---|---|---|---|---|---|
| | I. LEADERSHIP AND VISION | II. LEARNING AND TEACHING | III. PRODUCTIVITY AND PROFESSIONAL PRACTICE | IV. SUPPORT, MANAGEMENT, AND OPERATIONS | V. ASSESSMENT AND EVALUATION | VI. SOCIAL, LEGAL, AND ETHICAL ISSUES |
| Education Commission of the States: Finance www.ecs.org/ecsmain.asp?page=/html/issuesK12.asp | | | | X | | |
| Education Finance Database www.ncsl.org/programs/educ/ed_finance/ | | | | X | | |
| Education Finance Statistics Center Publications nces.ed.gov/edfin/publications/pubs.asp | | | | X | | X |
| Federal, State, and Local Governments Public Elementary-Secondary Education Finance Data www.census.gov/govs/www/school.html | | | | X | | |
| Grants and Contests techlearning.com/resources/grants.jhtml | | | | X | | |
| School Finance: From Equity to Adequacy www.mcrel.org/PDF/PolicyBriefs/5042PI_PBSchoolFinanceBrief.pdf | | | | X | | X |
| School Finance Project www.wcer.wisc.edu/cpre/finance/ | | | | X | | |
| School Fund-Raising Activities That Work teacher.scholastic.com/professional/grants/school_fund_raising.htm | | | | X | | |
| SchoolGrants www.schoolgrants.org | | | | X | | |
| U.S. Department of Education: Budget Office www.ed.gov/about/overview/budget/index.html?src=gu | | | | X | | X |

# NETS•A CORRELATION MATRIX: GENERAL

| NAME OF SITE/INTERNET ADDRESS | STANDARDS | | | | | |
|---|---|---|---|---|---|---|
| | I. LEADERSHIP AND VISION | II. LEARNING AND TEACHING | III. PRODUCTIVITY AND PROFESSIONAL PRACTICE | IV. SUPPORT, MANAGEMENT, AND OPERATIONS | V. ASSESSMENT AND EVALUATION | VI. SOCIAL, LEGAL, AND ETHICAL ISSUES |
| AOL@School Administrators www.aolatschool.com/administrators/ | ■ | ■ | ■ | | | |
| Clearinghouse on Educational Policy and Management (CEPM) eric.uoregon.edu | ■ | ■ | ■ | ■ | ■ | ■ |
| e-Lead: Leadership for Student Learning www.e-lead.org | ■ | ■ | ■ | ■ | ■ | |
| National Library of Education www.ed.gov/NLE/ | | ■ | ■ | ■ | | |
| School Administrators Center www.education-world.com/a_admin/ | ■ | ■ | | ■ | ■ | ■ |
| TeAch-nology www.teach-nology.com/edleadership/ | ■ | ■ | | | ■ | ■ |
| U.S. Department of Education www.ed.gov | ■ | ■ | | ■ | ■ | ■ |

# NETS•A CORRELATION MATRIX: INSTRUCTION

| NAME OF SITE/INTERNET ADDRESS | STANDARDS | | | | | |
|---|---|---|---|---|---|---|
| | I. LEADERSHIP AND VISION | II. LEARNING AND TEACHING | III. PRODUCTIVITY AND PROFESSIONAL PRACTICE | IV. SUPPORT, MANAGEMENT, AND OPERATIONS | V. ASSESSMENT AND EVALUATION | VI. SOCIAL, LEGAL, AND ETHICAL ISSUES |
| About Learning<br>www.funderstanding.com/about_learning.cfm | | ▓ | | | | |
| Big6<br>big6.com | | ▓ | | | | |
| Block Scheduling<br>education.umn.edu/carei/blockscheduling/ | | ▓ | | | | |
| Filamentality<br>www.kn.sbc.com/wired/fil/ | | ▓ | ▓ | | | |
| Introduction to Teaching Strategies<br>www.aea267.k12.ia.us/cia/framework/strategies/ | | ▓ | | | | |
| Landmarks for Schools<br>landmark-project.com | | ▓ | ▓ | | | |
| Leadership by Walking Around: Walkthroughs and Instructional Improvement<br>www.principalspartnership.com/feature203.html | | ▓ | | | ▓ | |
| NCRTEC Lesson Planner<br>www.ncrtec.org/tl/lp/ | | ▓ | | | | |
| School Libraries & You: Administrators & School Board Members<br>www.ala.org/ala/aasl/schlibrariesandyou/administrators/schoollibraries.htm | | ▓ | | | | |

# NETS•A CORRELATION MATRIX: PERSONAL PRODUCTIVITY

| NAME OF SITE/INTERNET ADDRESS | STANDARDS | | | | | |
| --- | --- | --- | --- | --- | --- | --- |
| | I. LEADERSHIP AND VISION | II. LEARNING AND TEACHING | III. PRODUCTIVITY AND PROFESSIONAL PRACTICE | IV. SUPPORT, MANAGEMENT, AND OPERATIONS | V. ASSESSMENT AND EVALUATION | VI. SOCIAL, LEGAL, AND ETHICAL ISSUES |
| Adobe Reader www.adobe.com/products/acrobat/ readermain.html | | | ▓ | | | |
| Backflip www.backflip.com | | | ▓ | | | |
| In and Out of the Classroom www.microsoft.com/education/ ?ID=IOCTutorials | | | ▓ | | | |
| Internet Search Tools Quick Reference Guide www.itrc.ucf.edu/conferences/pres/ srchtool.html | | | ▓ | | | |
| Pdf995 www.pdf995.com/suite.html | | | ▓ | | | |

# NETS•A CORRELATION MATRIX: PROFESSIONAL DEVELOPMENT

| NAME OF SITE/INTERNET ADDRESS | STANDARDS | | | | | |
|---|---|---|---|---|---|---|
| | I. LEADERSHIP AND VISION | II. LEARNING AND TEACHING | III. PRODUCTIVITY AND PROFESSIONAL PRACTICE | IV. SUPPORT, MANAGEMENT, AND OPERATIONS | V. ASSESSMENT AND EVALUATION | VI. SOCIAL, LEGAL, AND ETHICAL ISSUES |
| Career-Long Teacher Development: Policies That Make Sense www.wested.org/cs/we/view/rs/469 | ■ | ■ | | | | |
| Concept to Classroom: A Series of Workshops www.thirteen.org/edonline/concept2class | | ■ | ■ | | | |
| Edutopia Online: Professional Development www.glef.org | ■ | ■ | | | | |
| Financing Professional Development in Education www.financeprojectinfo.org/ProfDevelop/Wallace.asp | | ■ | | ■ | | |
| Linking Staff Development to Student Learning www.mcrel.org/toolkit/process/ex-prof.asp | | ■ | | | | |
| Professional Development: Learning From the Best www.ncrel.org/pd/toolkit.htm | ■ | ■ | | | | |

# NETS•A CORRELATION MATRIX: PROFESSIONAL ORGANIZATIONS

| NAME OF SITE/INTERNET ADDRESS | STANDARDS | | | | | |
| --- | --- | --- | --- | --- | --- | --- |
| | I. LEADERSHIP AND VISION | II. LEARNING AND TEACHING | III. PRODUCTIVITY AND PROFESSIONAL PRACTICE | IV. SUPPORT, MANAGEMENT, AND OPERATIONS | V. ASSESSMENT AND EVALUATION | VI. SOCIAL, LEGAL, AND ETHICAL ISSUES |
| American Association of School Administrators (AASA) www.aasa.org | ■ | | | | ■ | |
| Association for Supervision and Curriculum Development (ASCD) www.ascd.org | ■ | | | | ■ | |
| International Society for Technology in Education (ISTE) www.iste.org | ■ | ■ | ■ | ■ | ■ | ■ |
| National Association of Elementary School Principals (NAESP) www.naesp.org | ■ | | | | ■ | |
| National Association of Secondary School Principals (NASSP) www.nassp.org | ■ | | | | ■ | |
| National Middle School Association (NMSA) www.nmsa.org | ■ | | | | ■ | |
| National Staff Development Council (NSDC) www.nsdc.org | | ■ | | | | |

# NETS•A CORRELATION MATRIX: PROFESSIONAL READING

| NAME OF SITE/INTERNET ADDRESS | STANDARDS | | | | | |
|---|---|---|---|---|---|---|
| | I. LEADERSHIP AND VISION | II. LEARNING AND TEACHING | III. PRODUCTIVITY AND PROFESSIONAL PRACTICE | IV. SUPPORT, MANAGEMENT, AND OPERATIONS | V. ASSESSMENT AND EVALUATION | VI. SOCIAL, LEGAL, AND ETHICAL ISSUES |
| ASCD's SmartBrief www.smartbrief.com/ascd/ | ▨ | ▨ | | | ▨ | ▨ |
| The Doyle Report www.thedoylereport.com | ▨ | ▨ | | | ▨ | ▨ |
| Ed Week Update www.edweek.org | ▨ | ▨ | | | ▨ | ▨ |
| eSchool News This Week www.eschoolnews.com/emailprofile/ | ▨ | ▨ | | | ▨ | ▨ |
| PEN Weekly NewsBlast www.publiceducation.org | | ▨ | | | ▨ | ▨ |
| Phi Delta Kappan www.pdkintl.org/kappan/kappan.htm | ▨ | ▨ | | | | |
| Reading Online www.readingonline.org | | ▨ | ▨ | | ▨ | |
| Scholastic Administr@tor www.scholastic.com/administrator/ | ▨ | ▨ | | | ▨ | |
| School Administrator www.aasa.org/publications/sa/ | ▨ | ▨ | | ▨ | | ▨ |
| Technology and Learning Magazine www.techlearning.com/content/about/ tl_current.html | ▨ | ▨ | ▨ | ▨ | ▨ | ▨ |
| Today's School www.peterli.com/ts/ | ▨ | ▨ | ▨ | ▨ | ▨ | ▨ |

# NETS•A CORRELATION MATRIX:
# RESEARCH INSTITUTES AND EDUCATION CENTERS

| NAME OF SITE/INTERNET ADDRESS | STANDARDS | | | | | |
|---|---|---|---|---|---|---|
| | I. LEADERSHIP AND VISION | II. LEARNING AND TEACHING | III. PRODUCTIVITY AND PROFESSIONAL PRACTICE | IV. SUPPORT, MANAGEMENT, AND OPERATIONS | V. ASSESSMENT AND EVALUATION | VI. SOCIAL, LEGAL, AND ETHICAL ISSUES |
| Annenberg Institute for School Reform<br>www.annenberginstitute.org | ▓ | | | | ▓ | |
| Appalachia Educational Laboratory (AEL)<br>www.ael.org | ▓ | ▓ | | | | |
| The Education Alliance at Brown University<br>www.alliance.brown.edu | ▓ | ▓ | | | | ▓ |
| Institute of Education Sciences (IES )<br>www.ed.gov/about/offices/list/ies/<br>index.html?src=mr | ▓ | | | ▓ | ▓ | |
| Laboratory for Student Success (LSS),<br>Mid-Atlantic Regional Educational Laboratory<br>www.temple.edu/LSS/ | ▓ | ▓ | | | | |
| Mid-continent Research for Education and<br>Learning (McREL)<br>www.mcrel.org | ▓ | ▓ | | | ▓ | |
| North Central Regional Educational Laboratory<br>(NCREL)<br>www.ncrel.org | ▓ | ▓ | | | | |
| Northwest Regional Educational Laboratory<br>(NWREL)<br>www.nwrel.org | ▓ | ▓ | | | | |
| Pacific Resources for Education and Learning<br>(PREL)<br>www.prel.org | ▓ | ▓ | | | ▓ | |
| RAND Education<br>www.rand.org/education/ | ▓ | ▓ | | | ▓ | |
| Southeast Regional Vision for Education<br>(SERVE)<br>www.serve.org | ▓ | ▓ | ▓ | | ▓ | |
| Southwest Educational Development Laboratory<br>(SEDL)<br>www.sedl.org | ▓ | ▓ | | | | |
| WestEd<br>www.wested.org | ▓ | ▓ | | | ▓ | |

# NETS•A CORRELATION MATRIX: SOCIAL AND LEGAL ISSUES

| NAME OF SITE/INTERNET ADDRESS | STANDARDS | | | | | |
|---|---|---|---|---|---|---|
| | I.<br>LEADERSHIP<br>AND VISION | II.<br>LEARNING<br>AND<br>TEACHING | III.<br>PRODUCTIVITY<br>AND<br>PROFESSIONAL<br>PRACTICE | IV.<br>SUPPORT,<br>MANAGEMENT,<br>AND<br>OPERATIONS | V.<br>ASSESSMENT<br>AND<br>EVALUATION | VI.<br>SOCIAL,<br>LEGAL, AND<br>ETHICAL<br>ISSUES |
| Center for the Prevention of School Violence (CPSV)<br>www.ncdjjdp.org/cpsv/ | | | | | | |
| Federal Register<br>www.gpoaccess.gov/fr/ | | | | | | |
| NEA Crisis Communications Guide & Toolkit<br>www.nea.org/crisis/ | | | | | | |
| Office of Special Education and Rehabilitative Services<br>www.ed.gov/about/offices/list/osers/osep/ | | | | | | |

# NETS•A CORRELATION MATRIX: TECHNOLOGY USE

| NAME OF SITE/INTERNET ADDRESS | STANDARDS | | | | | |
|---|---|---|---|---|---|---|
| | I. LEADERSHIP AND VISION | II. LEARNING AND TEACHING | III. PRODUCTIVITY AND PROFESSIONAL PRACTICE | IV. SUPPORT, MANAGEMENT, AND OPERATIONS | V. ASSESSMENT AND EVALUATION | VI. SOCIAL, LEGAL, AND ETHICAL ISSUES |
| Center for Applied Research in Educational Technology (CARET) **caret.iste.org** | ● | ● | | | ● | |
| Consortium for School Networking (CoSN) **www.cosn.org** | ● | | | ● | | |
| Educator's Reference Desk: Educational Technology **www.eduref.org/cgi-bin/res.cgi/ Educational_Technology** | ● | ● | ● | ● | ● | ● |
| Network of Regional Technology in Education Consortia (R*TEC) **www.rtec.org** | ● | ● | ● | ● | ● | ● |
| Partnership for 21st Century Skills **www.21stcenturyskills.org** | ● | ● | | | | |
| Pew Internet & American Life Project **www.pewinternet.org** | ● | ● | | | | ● |
| Technology Information Center for Administrative Leadership (TICAL) **www.portical.org** | ● | ● | ● | ● | ● | ● |

# Glossary

Techies are a lot like educators when it comes to vocabulary: they tend to use many acronyms and terms nontechnology users don't recognize. One hurdle to becoming a proficient Internet user is simply learning the language. The following glossary includes the basic terms used in chapters 1–4.

**adware.** See spyware.

**back door.** A program that runs secretly on a computer, opening a hole in its security that allows outsiders access to the system.

**browser hijackers.** Spyware programs that change your Internet browser settings, such as your home page or bookmark list, without your consent.

**cable modem.** A modem designed to send and receive data through television cable networks. Data transmission speed is very fast. This service is not available in all areas through all cable companies.

**domain name.** A domain name is part of an Internet address, or URL. It locates on the Internet an organization or other entity that owns the Web site. The domain name provides information on the origin of a Web page, helping educators determine a page's credibility.

**DSL.** Short for digital subscriber line. DSL offers subscribers a high-speed Internet connection through telephone lines. DSL is not available in all areas and is dependent upon subscribers' proximity to telephone switching stations.

**firewall.** Hardware or software that protects a computer system from intrusion. It prevents unauthorized access by filtering every packet of information coming in from or going out to the Internet and blocking any traffic that does not meet its security criteria.

**home page.** The main page of a Web site.

**Internet.** The Internet provides the network infrastructure that enables millions of computers around the world to connect to one another for communication purposes.

**ISP.** Short for Internet service provider. These companies provide access to the Internet for a monthly fee. A dial-up connection to the Internet requires that a user go through an ISP to access the Internet.

**keylogger.** A program that runs secretly on a computer, tracking every keystroke that a user makes and sending that information back to its creator. Keyloggers are most often used to steal credit card numbers, passwords, or other personal information.

**malware.** A generic term for malicious software. Programs of this type are intention ally designed to damage computer files or disrupt normal system and network operations.

**modem.** Stands for **mo**dulator-**dem**odulator. This device may be external (outside your computer) or internal (usually a card plugged into a slot inside your computer). The modem converts data stored on your computer into a format that can be transferred via telephone or cable lines. Different modems send and receive data at different speeds. Generally, the faster the better.

**search engine.** A program that searches files for specified keywords and produces a list of files containing the keywords. Although the term refers to a type of program, people generally use the term to refer to such Web sites as Google, Alta Vista, or Excite, which use such programs to search for files on the Internet.

**spoofing.** A technique used by hackers to gain unauthorized access to a computer or network share by imitating a trusted source in an e-mail message or on a Web site.

**spyware.** Software that gathers data about you and the way you use your computer, usually for commercial purposes. Often referred to as adware.

**Trojan horse.** Named after the gift horse of Trojan War fame, this is malware that masquerades as a free game or useful utility program. Once it is downloaded onto your computer, however, it can unleash a worm or keylogger or open a backdoor into your system.

**URL.** An abbreviation for Uniform Resource Locator. Every file on the Internet has a unique address, or URL, assigned to it so that you can find the file. URLs have two parts. The first part identifies the protocol, or format, of the file. Most Web page

URLs begin with "http." The second part of the URL is the domain name, which identifies where the Web page you want is stored (see definition for *domain name*).

**virus.** A piece of computer code that can replicate itself once it has found a host (your computer). A virus can be downloaded without your knowledge and execute or run itself without your permission.

**Web browser.** This is a software program (application) used to access Web pages. The two most commonly used Web browsers are Internet Explorer and Netscape Navigator.

**Web directory.** A list of categories and subcategories you can browse to find Web sites. It's most helpful when you're looking for general information.

**World Wide Web.** The World Wide Web is one source of information for Internet users, but it is not the Internet itself. It uses the Internet network to allow people to access Web sites.

**worm.** A computer program that roams networks autonomously, bogging computers down by using up available memory, destroying files, stealing passwords and credit card numbers, and opening backdoors on infected systems.